SEOUL
SUB→URBAN

Seoul Sub→urban

Copyright © 2017 by Charles Usher
All Rights Reserved
No part of this book may be reproduced or utilized in any form or by any
means without the written permission of the publisher.

Published in 2017 by Seoul Selection U.S.A., Inc.
4199 Campus Drive, Suite 550, Irvine, CA 92612

Phone: 949-509-6584 / Seoul office: 82-2-734-9567
Fax: 949-509-6599 / Seoul office: 82-2-734-9562
Email: planner@seoulselection.com

ISBN: 978-1-62412-084-8
Library of Congress Control Number: 2017931684

Printed in the Republic of Korea

SEOUL
SUB→URBAN

Charles Usher

Seoul Selection

CONTENTS

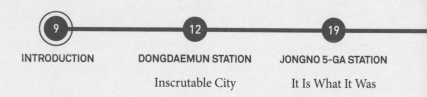
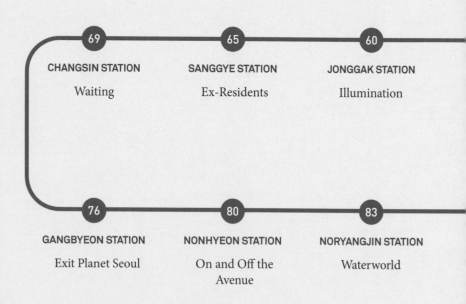

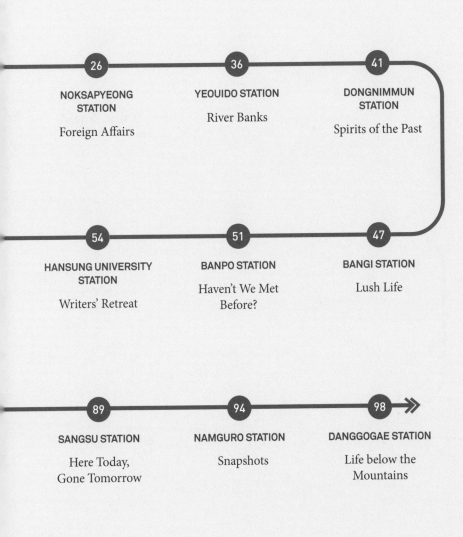

26 NOKSAPYEONG STATION

Foreign Affairs

36 YEOUIDO STATION

River Banks

41 DONGNIMMUN STATION

Spirits of the Past

54 HANSUNG UNIVERSITY STATION

Writers' Retreat

51 BANPO STATION

Haven't We Met Before?

47 BANGI STATION

Lush Life

89 SANGSU STATION

Here Today, Gone Tomorrow

94 NAMGURO STATION

Snapshots

98 DANGGOGAE STATION

Life below the Mountains

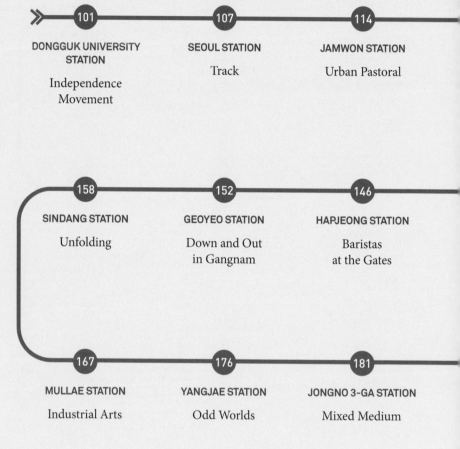

101
DONGGUK UNIVERSITY STATION

Independence Movement

107
SEOUL STATION

Track

114
JAMWON STATION

Urban Pastoral

158
SINDANG STATION

Unfolding

152
GEOYEO STATION

Down and Out in Gangnam

146
HAPJEONG STATION

Baristas at the Gates

167
MULLAE STATION

Industrial Arts

176
YANGJAE STATION

Odd Worlds

181
JONGNO 3-GA STATION

Mixed Medium

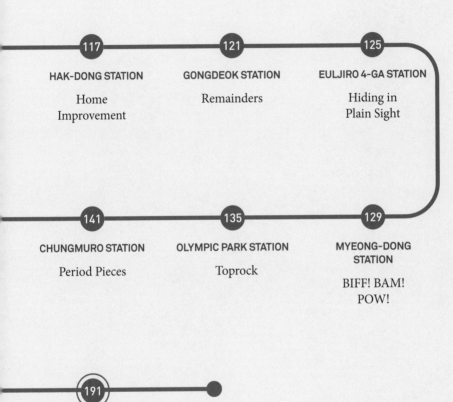

INTRODUCTION

When I first moved to Seoul, in 2005, whenever I rode the subway and the train pulled into a new station the same thought would creep up: *What if I just got off here? What's up there?* Though I imagined this new city was full of discoveries, I soon found myself constrained by habit, stuck shuttling between the same handful of neighborhoods where I lived, worked, and played. I knew I was missing things, though what, exactly, I wasn't sure.

We travel—or move halfway around the world—for the sense of discovery it gives us, to feel the exuberant shiver of raw experience, of the transformation from not knowing to knowing. Too often, though, we neglect the discoveries available to us in the place we live, even if that place is an ocean apart from home. Sooner or later a sense of ennui sets in, preventing us from really knowing our surroundings. Besides this more universal inertia, other factors add to Seoul's specific inscrutability, rendering it harder to know than most cities. There's its sheer size, making a thorough reckoning difficult, and there's the way Seoul cloaks itself in its fast pace. Things change so quickly and there's so much pressure to keep up that residents are forced into a lifestyle of constant movement, and the city becomes something ever-present yet incidental, like the blur of scenery out the window of a high-speed train. On top of these factors, those who aren't natives must deal with the language barrier and the often thick line that Korean culture draws between Koreans and outsiders.

My relationship with Seoul was casual the first time I lived here, and when I made the decision to move back in 2009 I also made the decision to try to get to know it better. And the only way to do that was to do what I hadn't done before: get off the train and look for answers to my questions. Thus, the Seoul Sub→urban project (seoulsuburban.com) was born. I began visiting random subway stations across the capital, trying to look at parts of Seoul—both those I'd never been to and those I'd already visited countless times—more deliberately, more closely, and from new perspectives. The project has taken me to over 160 stations, a selection of which is collected here, and has explored everything from downtown tourist centers to obscure neighborhoods that even most Seoulites know little about. It has taken me to traditional markets, ancient historical sites, industrial zones, and the city's trendiest neighborhoods. It's also given me a chance to meet some of the people who live in those places and who make Seoul the vibrant city it is: market vendors, artists, blacksmiths, and others.

Like Korea and Koreans, Seoul is constantly changing, trying to figure out what it is and what it wants to be, and it's this dynamism and unpredictability that, while making the city difficult to know, also make it so fascinating. The Korean capital is endlessly complex, and understanding it takes time and dogged perseverance. The fact that the latter is a defining trait of the country's people perhaps lends a bit of teeth-gritted poetry to the city—to begin to know it you must do so on its own, Korean terms. Only when you've done this will Seoul open up and share its endless tiny revelations, though when it does it will do so only to offer more questions. But that's the reward. Like in the best romances, the mystery is never lost. The city is never figured out; the sense of discovery never disappears.

INSCRUTABLE CITY

Slow revelations in Seoul's most beguiling neighborhood

It begins the moment I step off the subway. There, on the platform, a man calls out to passengers, hawking the belts curled
up in compartmentalized boxes at his feet, and before exiting
the station I've passed a half dozen others doing the same—
with bags, with clothes, with battery-operated toys that flash and
clatter—all of which serves as mere prelude to what surrounds
me when I reach the top of the stairs and find myself, yet again,
in Dongdaemun. Acres of wholesale markets pull in old-timers
in search of bargains, while the malls that are the wellspring
of Korean fashion summon the young and style-conscious.
Sleek stores and developments coexist amicably with the gritty
shops and restaurants that have occupied the innumerable back
alleys for decades. Dongdaemun combines the crustiness of the

dockyards with the pulsing strut of the catwalk. Nowhere else in Seoul is quite like it. The neighborhood has always been one of my favorite places in the city to go, and yet it's also one of the most vexing. No matter how many times I return I always feel as if I'm missing something, unaware of some essential part of the neighborhood. Two eyes feel insufficient; each moment, each scene here feels so full of activity and movement that even Argus couldn't fully comprehend what was around him.

The one thing in the neighborhood that I feel I can hold fast to is the eponymous gate, more formally known as Heunginjimun, "Gate of Rising Benevolence." One of Joseon-era (1392–1910) Seoul's four main gates, it was originally built in 1396, though the current structure is an 1869 reconstruction. Besides being a beautiful example of traditional Korean architecture, it's a faithful reference point amid the hectic surroundings, an anchor in a bewildering sea.

After the gate, what the Dongdaemun area is most closely associated with is fashion. For decades, this has been where people have come to design, create, and wear the latest styles. Those aspiring to follow in the impeccably shod footsteps of André Kim (1935–2010), the first Korean designer to truly make a mark on the international scene, can head to Dongdaemun Fashion Town, where no supply goes wanting. Bolts of fabric are stacked like logs felled from a Technicolor forest; spools of ribbon and lace line up in rows; and buttons, clasps, and hooks are sorted into hundreds of boxes like artifacts at an archaeological dig.

If you prefer letting others do the work for you, the many iterations of Pyeonghwa Market running along the opposite side of the Cheonggyecheon Stream offer myriad clothing shops. There's also luggage, fishing supplies, and God knows what else. I've ventured in to explore these markets on several occasions, but every

time I find their interiors so indecipherable, the merchandise so disparate that I give up trying to make any sense of them and retreat back outside.

Behind the Pyeonghwa buildings, on either side of Heung-inmun-ro, a group of retail and wholesale malls cluster, each with floor after floor of everything from cheap, mass-produced T-shirts to designer goods. With so many places offering so much, it's useful (and almost necessary) that many of these malls stay open virtually all night. And indeed, to experience the full force of the scene's energy it's best to visit on a weekend night, when shoppers pack the boutiques and sidewalks, K-pop blasts into the air, and high school students lip-synch and perform dance routines on the outdoor stages. It all makes the night come alive in ways that are impressive even by Seoul's nocturnal standards. If I have the energy, it's one of my favorite times and places to shop, and if it gets to be too much, sometimes I'll just sit on a café patio and watch the crowds: couples out on shopping dates; college students hunting for cheap threads; Chinese, Thai, and Vietnamese tour groups piling back onto their buses, the pendulums of bags in their hands bumping against the doorframes as they board.

There's no shortage to the non-clothing shopping that can be done in Dongdaemun, either, much of it wonderfully idiosyncratic. Just in front of the clothing malls and parallel to the Cheonggyecheon Stream, used booksellers persevere, selling their well-worn tomes from spaces often barely bigger than a walk-in closet. Further east and on the north side of the stream is the market's shoe section, where store after store sells everything from sneakers to high heels, with many on display in protective plastic shells. Beyond the shoe stores is the market's most exotic stretch, an area of pet shops specializing in aquariums and more uncommon fauna. A late afternoon stroll through the area will reveal hundreds of goldfish glinting bright saffron in the setting sun, while the nervous prattle and coo of songbirds fills the air. You can also find kittens, turtles, rabbits, hamsters, hedgehogs, ferrets, iguanas, roosters, chickens, ducks, parakeets, finches, and cockatiels here. North of the pet market is a warren of backstreets where more aquarium shops are interspersed with barebones restaurants offering back-alley foods like dog stew and *seolleong-tang*, or ox-bone soup. Further in, the area is home to a sprawling toy market, making this potentially the most treacherous square kilometer in Seoul for parents of small children.

The bulk of Dongdaemun's shopping areas are south of the gate, but the area to the north is also intriguing and dense. Keeping your eyes open rewards you with a series of the one-of-a-kind images that this part of town always provides. Elderly Korean women with kerchiefs tied to their heads sell peeled garlic outside Nike stores. Mobile carts selling tapes and CDs blare old Korean pop music. Porters lug goods about on their backs, using carriers that look like miniature wooden chairs missing front legs. A man in a suit and tie pedaling a delivery trishaw loaded down with sacks of beans passes by.

Seoul's older neighborhoods often have its best restaurants, and the timeworn backstreets of Dongdaemun offer fertile hunting grounds. In the mood one evening for something gritty and greasy and preferably served up by an old woman with an ill disposition, I looked down a side alley and spotted a sign displaying a disembodied hand holding the tail of a deep red, dangling pig. The sign, location, and simple metal door looked perfect. The restaurant's name is a bit hard to translate, but Wageul Wageul Jokbal means something like "Boisterous Pork Trotters," and this too seemed to encapsulate the irreverent, guileless atmosphere that typifies both trotter restaurants and Dongdaemun itself. Inside was a bit of a surprise, however. I had expected floors sticky with grease and a clientele whose ages ran mostly north of 60, but Wageul Wageul was clean, well-lit, and filled with a mix of 20-somethings and stylish middle-agers. Its niceness actually made me question whether the trotters would be any good. A second look around eased my worries as, despite the nicer-than-expected surroundings, the place clearly held no pretensions, and with tongues lubricated by alcohol and pig fat, the clientele provided an ambiance befitting the joint's name. The trotters I was served sealed the deal.

Occasionally no amount of good food or compelling sights can prevent the Dongdaemun Experience from getting to be just a bit too much. At times like these, the area's best escape hatch is the Naksan Trail leading up to Naksan Park, where, after just a few dozen meters, the neighborhood's bustle diminishes. The trail up and out follows either side of the reconstructed old city wall. On the east side, things are tidy. The path is paved and speakers play music ranging from classical to the old "Cheers" theme song. The path on the west side is rougher, but while the eastern one lies below the wall, here it runs even, letting you look out over Dongdaemun and appreciate its commotion without being subjected to it.

Dongdaemun, in its size and scope, can be overwhelming, and any attempts to understand or even see all of it in one trip (or 10) will only end in disappointment. In that way it's a microcosm of life in Seoul, the great, inscrutable city—answers and understanding are hard to come by, which can frustrate, but that intrigue is also a large part of Seoul's power, and Dongdaemun's. You always feel like you're missing something, but as long as you persist in coming back, this endlessly fascinating place will keep revealing new secrets, surprising every time.

Key places: Dongdaemun Gate (Heunginjimun Gate), Dongdaemun Fashion Town, Cheonggyecheon Stream, Pyeonghwa Market,
fashion malls, used booksellers, shoe and pet markets, toy market,
Wageul Wageul Jokbal, Naksan Trail and Naksan Park

IT IS WHAT IT WAS

Where today is back in the day

Waiting on a downtown platform for the Line 1 train, a friend once made an offhand remark about just how different the Line 1 is from the other lines of the Seoul metro. Its stations and riders are older and more worn, but, as he pointed out, it's not just inside the stations that you notice the difference; the parts of town along the line feel different too. Since Line 1 was the first to be built, it was designed to cut through Seoul's focal points at the time. Trace the first section that opened, in 1974, and it runs from Seoul Station along the main downtown avenue of Jongno, and through Dongdaemun Market before terminating at Cheongnyangni Station. Despite how much most of Seoul has modernized in the 40 years since, large parts of these areas have not—buildings are older, major traditional markets fall along this line, and there's a mustiness that clings to the neighborhoods like moss.

All of which, really, is fine by me. It's those areas, after all, that tend to reward a day of exploration the most.

In front of a long string of pharmacies on Jongno, some of which predate Line 1 by a good 20 years, I passed one man selling three different varieties of dried shrimp from a large wheeled cart and another squatting on the sidewalk, letting the long ash from his cigarette fall onto the bag of bananas between his feet. In the backstreets north of the station, the old women that are fixtures of Seoul's restaurant kitchens sat around waiting for customers. There were metal shops and a warehouse where many coils of ribbed black plastic tubing were stacked up, and a couple traditional tile-roofed wood homes hidden in the alleys. In an empty lot, construction workers were gathered around a table, eating and pouring *makgeolli*, a milky rice wine, and a bit further east was a slew of bars and restaurants, most serving up solidly working-class fare like catfish soup, fermented skate, potato and pork bone stew, and grilled intestines. Down Daehak-ro 2-gil, among several inns and karaoke parlors, half-naked women stood in the glass windows of hostess bars. Unlike similar places I'd seen throughout the city, these seemed targeted at an older clientele—the women were in their forties, and several establishments were places where a hostess would entertain customers by playing the *janggu*, an hourglass-shaped drum, or *gayageum*, a 12-stringed zither. Macabrely, several of the signs advertised widows.

Even in an area like Jongno 5-ga, though, gentrification is inevitably creeping in, changing the neighborhood's character coffee shop by coffee shop and more drastically with places like the Doosan Art Center. There, smartly dressed 20-somethings sounded notes as they stepped on and off electric piano keys embedded in the floor and wandered in and out of a group painting and photography exhibition that hovered somewhere between the playful and the sinister. Matching red bronze sculptures—*Big Boy* and *Little Pig* by the Chinese artist Chen Wenling—greeted visitors making their way downstairs to see a performance of *Spring Awakening.*

Yet as Jongno 5-ga gradually transforms, its major landmark is unlikely to change, given its size and historical importance. Gwangjang Market has been doing business since 1905, making it the oldest continually operating market in the country. And since eating is such a central part of the Gwangjang experience, and no one in Korea eats alone if they can help it, I recruited a couple of friends to join me at a crowded stall for *bindaetteok*, a mung bean pancake that's Gwangjang's signature dish. While we ate, workers scooped mung beans onto a gently sloped spinning stone wheel that ground the beans into a smooth, pale-yellow paste. This was poured into a thin pool of oil on the griddle, and as the exterior acquired a golden crispness, the interior stayed soft, the consistency of a baked potato.

The collection of food stalls in the market's interior was huge, a parade of hot pepper and oil that ran up one aisle and down the next. Hundreds of fluorescent bulbs hanging from the curved metal roof lit stall after stall filled with the Korean street stand holy trinity of chewy *tteokbokki* (rice cakes in a spicy sauce), *twigim* (Korean tempura), and long tubes of *sundae* (blood sausage), twice as thick as any I've seen elsewhere. A woman at one stall was hand-cutting made-from-scratch noodles, while an old man nearby sharpened knives on a hand-turned whetstone.

Gwangjang isn't just eateries. It's a regular wet market as well, and for more than half its existence, the Hongrim shop has been there selling *banchan*, the assorted side dishes that are an indispensable part of every Korean meal. Kim Sun-ok and her husband run the stall, which belonged to her mother-in-law when she first began working there nearly four decades ago. A petite woman with an easy smile, she looked vaguely familiar, though initially I couldn't quite figure out why.

Two dozen different kinds of *banchan* filled square metal containers at the front of the stall, some of which Kim had bought from people living in the countryside and some of which she had made herself. I'd assumed that with the rise of the big conglomerate-owned supermarkets that vendors in Gwangjang would have seen business suffer, but Kim felt that wasn't entirely the case.

"They've hurt business a little, but traditional markets have their own beauty, so people still like to come here for that," she told me. As her husband measured and scooped up pickled radishes beneath a picture of a Korean bishop, Kim claimed that, in a way, modernization had actually helped her business. "Thirty-five years ago the eating culture was different and people made food themselves. Now they buy food outside, so in that way business is better. Back then, no one really thought to buy kimchi outside. It was quite unusual."

I wasn't entirely convinced by Kim's spin, as several neighborhood markets in Seoul had closed in recent years, but it was nice to hope that it might be true, both for her and for the city, which was pushing to revitalize the markets that were left. Near the end of our conversation, Kim also revealed why she looked so familiar. I *had* seen her before, all over the city in fact—on the sides of newsstands and rolling by on buses—posing in front of her *banchan* shop as part of Seoul's PR campaign to bring shoppers back to the markets.

Besides food, Gwangjang is best known as a place to buy *hanbok*, traditional clothing made of silk or ramie. While the fabric itself is produced elsewhere, often in the southern cities of Jinju and Daegu, much of what is shipped to Seoul makes its way here, where it's sold in shops like Lim Ji-yeong Uri Ot, where Song Myeong-sun works. From behind a glass case filled with cloth butterflies and other detailing, Song explained that after choosing their fabric, customers take their purchase upstairs, where tailors on the third and fourth floors turn it into the billowing skirts and low-hanging sleeves that give *hanbok* its distinctive silhouette.

It's a silhouette that's rarely seen anymore. Even Song wasn't wearing *hanbok*, dressed instead in a simple black cotton dress that contrasted sharply with the hundreds of bolts of colorful fabric arrayed on shelves around her.

"I do wear it sometimes," she told me, "but not in summer and only a vest and only at work."

The expense of having a suit made and the style's impracticality for everyday wear have largely relegated *hanbok* to the status of prop. After a wedding—during which bride and groom typically wear a Western dress and suit—newlyweds will change into *hanbok* for the reception, and a few more traditionally minded families will don it for the fall Chuseok harvest festival and the Lunar New Year, Korea's two biggest holidays, but it's otherwise become a casualty of Korea's modernization. A number of *hanbok* stores were still doing business in Gwangjang, though, and I asked Song who her customers were.

"It's mostly brides, moms, and grooms buying, but other than that there are people going to some religious events. Women wear *hanbok* for those, like on Easter and while doing charity work."

To try and adapt to changing customs, shops were also breaking from tradition, introducing new interpretations such as something Song called "modernized *hanbok*," made of rayon and dyed with natural dyes, which had become the shop's main item.

After our tour of Gwangjang and our working man's hors d'oeuvres, my friends and I set off for our real dinner. While exploring Dongdaemun on an earlier occasion, I'd stumbled across an alley of *dakhanmari* restaurants. After three-plus years in Korea it was the first I'd ever heard of the dish, and when I asked Korean friends about it they compared it to *samgyetang*, a soup containing a whole chicken stuffed with ginseng, garlic, and Korean dates. This didn't particularly encourage me, as *samgyetang* is one of the few Korean foods I don't care for—I find it bland and dull—but I wanted to give *dakhanmari* a shot nonetheless.

After the three of us ordered, a large metal bowl filled with water, potatoes, rice cakes, and onions was set on the burner in the middle of our table. One waitress then picked up the whole chicken that was also in the bowl (the dish's name literally means "one chicken") and used scissors to cut it into chunks while another mixed up a sauce consisting of garlic, chives, mustard, soy sauce, and red pepper paste. As it boiled, the chicken fat gave the broth a comfortingly oily consistency, reminding me of the golden droplets in my mom's homemade chicken noodle soup. But it was the sauce that made the meal. Dipping the boiled chicken and sliced onion in it was a revelation: distinctly Korean, yet not quite like anything any of us had ever had before, even though we'd all lived in the country for several years. It made me wonder why anyone would bother with *samgyetang* when there's *dakhanmari* to be had.

After saying goodnight to my friends, I decided to take a quick wander down to the Cheonggyecheon Stream. It's a peaceful scene there, far from its busy head near City Hall but not quite at the bustle of Dongdaemun's night markets, and the water flows slow and gentle. Crossing the street to get to the stream, I saw one of the most uncanny sights I'd ever witnessed in the city. Coming in the opposite direction, inch by painstaking inch, was an old woman barely more than a meter. Dressed in an all-white commoner's *hanbok*, she carried a simple bag and a polished branch that had been fashioned into a walking stick, taller than she was and twisted into a gnarled stub at the top like a wizard's staff. The image was absurd, something seemingly pulled from a Victorian travel diary, something I would have dismissed out of hand as unbelievable had I not seen it myself. As the woman took a full minute to cross a single lane, impervious and indifferent to the traffic she was holding up, her presence felt impossible, as if time had misplaced her. In Jongno, though, there's seldom a firm divide between the past and the present, and so there she was, among the high-rises and neon lights, undoubtedly, until I looked back a minute later and she was gone.

Key places: Doosan Art Center, Gwangjang Market, *dakhanmari* alley, Cheonggyecheon Stream

FOREIGN AFFAIRS

*How Seoul's most multicultural neighborhood
works, plays, and lives*

In the perfect center of Seoul is Mt. Namsan, and at its summit is
N Seoul Tower, from where tourists look out to panoramic views
of this megacity. If you go up after dusk, you'll notice a conspicu-
ous swath to the south where the sparkling metropolis has gone
almost completely dark. This is the Yongsan U.S. Army garrison,
and though it's not marked on Google Maps or any of the guides
handed out by tourism offices, it's most certainly there, sitting
right in the middle of the city.

Tucked between the mountain and the Hangang River, the
garrison occupies prime real estate, land whose strategic location
has seen it occupied by three different foreign armies throughout
its history. The Americans are just the latest, having moved in
following World War II. They've been there since, though a deal

is now in place for the U.S. Army to relocate its main base to Pyeongtaek, some 66 kilometers to the south, in 2017. The move's date has already been pushed back numerous times, and it may be pushed back again, but once it does happen the land will return to the citizens of Seoul, and the 2.5 square kilometers that make contemporary cartographers so eager to change the subject will return to the mapped world.

When you arrive in Noksapyeong, the first sign suggesting that certain neighbors are a bit more—let's say, private—than others is the tall brick and concrete walls topped with concertina wire that run along either side of Noksapyeong-daero, the area's north-south avenue. The menace is softened, though, by the ivy that climbs up the walls and over the coils, tall trees canopying the road, and flowers along the sidewalk. Behind the walls, the simple roofs look more academic than military, and were it not for the razor wire you might guess they formed a leafy college campus and not an army base. But pay attention and you'll notice the single police officers walking by at regular intervals or the "GO HOME" spray-painted on the sidewalk (in a frankly unconvincing seafoam green), reminding you that the neighbors wear camo and not tweed.

Few expats and even fewer Koreans get a chance to go on the base, which requires being the guest of a soldier or military staff member, but slip through the MP-patrolled rabbit hole, and it's as if you've landed in a small Midwestern town. The base itself is surprisingly pretty, with old and graceful buildings and more trees than you'll see most anywhere else in Seoul. But it was the smaller details that on my one visit hung me in a goofy limbo for three hours, caught between nostalgia and befuddlement: the transactions taking place in U.S. dollars, the smell of genuine Texas barbecue, the aging poster of Randall Cunningham taped to the wall outside the gym.

Even if you can't get on base, it's still worth coming down from the mountain and wandering around Noksapyeong, a neighborhood that for centuries has had a unique relationship with outsiders. Where once that relationship was defined by the presence of invading armies, it's now characterized by the recent influx of people from other countries looking to live and do business in Seoul, a foreign influence that has increasingly made the area feel like home for expats and like a taste of the exotic for Koreans.

Noksapyeong is well known among Seoulites for the large contingent of non-Koreans living there, and the neighborhood babbles with Korean, English, French, Arabic, Portuguese, and Yoruba. Many businesses cater to this diverse population, making things available here that can be tough to find elsewhere, like overseas call shops, Filipino grocers, and Western sports bars. The consequence is that Noksapyeong is sometimes pejoratively referred to as a foreigner ghetto. If there's any truth to this—and I find there's little—it's due simply to the fact that lots of expats have chosen to live near lots of other expats, as expats of every nationality tend to do all over the world, not because Koreans have chosen to pull out. In fact, large expat presence aside, the area ticks many of the boxes for what you'd want in an "authentic Korean neighborhood": plenty of mom-and-pop shops, simple restaurants, tailors, and dry cleaners.

Despite being an expat myself, until a couple of years ago Noksapyeong was never an area that I spent much time in. Just not my place. Recently, however, that's changed. And it's changed not only for me but for many others—both expat and native—as the area has transformed into one of the capital's hippest neighborhoods. With both the number of foreigners living in Seoul and the number of Koreans with cultural or economic ties abroad

increasing, Seoul's drinking and dining scene has kept apace, sprouting Western-style bakeries, cigar bars, and craft breweries, many of them in Noksapyeong. The area's newfound cachet has also had the predictable effect of luring in chain stores following the scent of money, and some of those mom-and-pop shops have been pushed out as a result.

As I started to come around more, these factors—the increasing cosmopolitanism, the new trendiness, the emerging corporate presence and the fact that local-expat dynamics are a constant topic in the foreign community—got me wondering about the relationship between the two groups. Korea was largely closed off to Westerners until the late 19th century, and Korean society still makes a plain distinction between those who are Korean and those who aren't. In a neighborhood with so many who aren't, did the two groups manage to get along?

Fortunately, it largely seems that they do. Dan Wilson, an Australian, and Kim Gi-nim, a local, run restaurants across an alley from each other—his a Greek gyro shop, hers a Korean barbecue joint—and both of them told me how much they liked the neighborhood's dynamic and running a business there. Kim's place was as good an example as any of how Noksapyeong functions, of the way that, owing to its familiarity with foreigners, it enables them to find a place in a tight-knit community more readily than other areas might. The walls of Kim's restaurant were lined with awards and certificates attesting to her husband's neighborhood volunteer work, and a young Chinese waitress tended to mid-afternoon customers. Her Korean wasn't perfect, and Kim interrupted our conversation briefly to help her out. The number of expats living and eating in the neighborhood had shot way up in the 10 years her restaurant had been open, but it was something she liked.

"The relationship with foreigners is pure," she said. "They're

honest. Everyone lives together and can learn something new."
While the expat demographic is global, Noksapyeong's Korean
demographic mostly divides along two lines. One, like Kim, is
the older working class—people who've lived and worked here
since long before foreigners started making the area their home.
The other is the young, cosmopolitan generation that's grown up
internationalized and that appreciates both Noksapyeong's globalized food and drink scene and the opportunity the area offers
to escape Korea's often rigid social structures.

A member of that second group who's also trying to capitalize
on it is Choi Su-yeon, whose Monster Cupcakes I came by while
walking down Hoenamu-ro, a road where Korean barbecue
joints share space with a whiskey bar and jerk chicken restaurant.
Choi used to live in the area back when the local foreigners were
mostly just military personnel. Now that Noksapyeong is more
diverse, she estimated that expats made up at least half of her
customers. Most of the rest, she said, were Koreans who weren't
from the area, or even from Seoul, but who came for the foreign
atmosphere, a pull that wasn't lost on Choi.

"I feel more comfortable here than in other neighborhoods,"
she said. "This area has more freedom. We can't smoke on the
street in other places, and here the clothing and fashion are
more free."

Between bites of lemon cupcake, I asked Choi about her
place's theme, unusual for a cupcake shop—it was filled with
old monster movie posters and other horror paraphernalia, and
American gangsta rap blared from the stereo. She laughed and
shrugged. "Well, I like it. And the concept fits here."

Besides food, natives and expats alike are increasingly coming
to Noksapyeong for its nightlife, drawn by an international
scene that's more subdued than in the neighboring Itaewon area.

They're also pulled in by bars that are rejecting the typical Korean view of drinks being simply a means to get drunk in favor of focusing on quality and craft.

A common complaint of expats in Korea is the low quality of domestic beer, and although I was spoiled growing up in Wisconsin, a state renowned for its breweries, I'm far from alone when I say that Korean beer is, to put it kindly, pitiable. I'm not sure if you can apply the adjective "scared" to beer, but that's exactly what Hite, Cass, and the rest of the domestic megabrews are: watery, bland, afraid to actually be real beer with anything resembling hops or flavor and to trust drinkers to learn what's good. Korean beer is, simply, some of the worst I've ever had. Actually, sorry, that's a bit unfair. I should clarify: *South* Korean beer is some of the worst I've had. I've drunk Taedonggang beer from the North and it's better, and not just by a little.

Despite the current sorry state, many, myself included, are optimistic. The last several years have witnessed a burgeoning craft brewing movement, spurred on by expat homebrewers and Koreans who've grown tired of the mass-produced domestic beer scene. Current legislation makes it difficult for small-batch brewers to bottle and distribute their products, making it challenging to become truly profitable, but should those barriers shift, the response from brewers would likely be immediate and profound. It's amazing what can happen when Koreans latch onto something. Take, for example, the transformation of Seoul's coffee scene. Ten years ago, coffee largely meant instant mixes and a few isolated Starbucks; now cafés are as ubiquitous as convenience stores, and some of the city's roasters and baristas create coffee as good as you'll have anywhere. Should Koreans' same single-minded perfectionism ever attach itself to beer, the results will be very, very good.

While we wait for the revolution, a number of fine microbreweries have opened over the past few years, and as Western expats have been at the vanguard of the movement, several of these are to be found in and around Noksapyeong, including Craftworks Taphouse & Bistro, one of the earliest and most successful. Though it now has multiple locations, the Noksapyeong branch was where the company first began selling the beers it made at its brewery in the town of Gapyeong, 55 kilometers northeast of Seoul. Once largely the preserve of the city's expats, the crowd sipping on Craftworks' IPAs, hefeweizens, and ales, each named after a Korean mountain, now features just as many born-and-bred Seoulites.

Across from Craftworks is a small road that runs past some kimchi pots into a neighborhood of steep streets and redbrick flats abutting the army base. The area is called Haebangchon—the name means "Freedom Village"—and it was founded by North Korean refugees in the wake of the Korean War. Nowadays it's probably the place with the densest foreign population in Seoul, its cheap rentals filled with English teachers, making it an unusual location for one of the city's other great watering holes.

Damotori [:h] specializes in *makgeolli*, a milky rice wine utterly unique to Korea. Traditionally the drink of farmers and long seen as an unfashionable peasant's brew, it's undergone a renaissance, and trendy bars serving *makgeolli* cocktails can now be found throughout the city. Eschewing the unnecessary dressing up, Damotori [:h] keeps it simple, focusing on the slightly sweet, slightly sour drink in its unadulterated form. Like wine, one of the biggest pleasures of drinking *makgeolli* is the variations it takes on according to where it was made, which is why Damotori [:h] is such an enjoyable place to drink—its some two dozen different kinds of *makgeolli* come from every one of Korea's mainland provinces, including one made from burnt glutinous rice from the eastern province of Gangwon-do province that's a personal favorite. Deep shamrock walls are paired with dark wood shelves displaying jars and cups in earth-toned glazes, and the music is kept low so the focus remains on the conversation and the drinks, which are served in heavy ceramic bottles. It's the kind of cozy neighborhood place where you could pass an entire night pouring cup after cup and swapping stories with old friends, which much of the clientele—balanced between Koreans and expats, in true Noksapyeong fashion—always seems intent on doing.

The chatty scene at Damotori [:h] reminded me of a woman I'd spoken to earlier in the neighborhood's Itaewon Market. Now 82, Park Geum-sun had several nights' worth of stories beneath the comb-over on her largely bald head, and she'd taken me through her years in Noksapyeong. When she was young, a building her family owned was torn down for a construction project; the meager compensation left the family too poor to do anything but open up a vegetable business in the market. Park said she'd worked since she was 27.

"At that time, there were no buildings, just trees and farms. The area was just mountains and animals running around, foxes catching chickens."

The U.S. army garrison was established, she got married, and her husband got a job working on the base. Now she worked with foreigners regularly too, and when several came through the market she put to use the simple English she had learned—names of vegetables, "one thousand," "bye."

Any changes that had occurred in the past 80 years, Park had seen, and now she was virtually a living almanac of Noksapyeong. I asked what she thought of the transformations the neighborhood had seen, and of the influx of foreign faces. She chuckled and answered me with an old Korean saying: "People live in people."

Key places: Yongsan U.S. Army Garrison, Craftworks Taphouse & Bistro, Damotori [:h]

Yeouido Station
Lines 5, 9

RIVER BANKS

(Almost) natural escapes in Korea's economic engine room

Change is a constant in Seoul, but few places in the city have evolved quite so dramatically as Yeouido. For much of the Joseon era (1392–1910) the island served as a sheep pasture, and that's pretty much how it stayed until the Japanese built the country's first airport there in the early 1900s. Still, it wasn't until the '70s and Korea's major industrialization that Yeouido began its transformation into a financial and political center. The island, whose name means "useless," owing to its formerly swampy terrain, is now the site of the national parliament, the headquarters of LG Electronics, Korea's largest megachurch, two of the country's major television networks, and numerous financial institutions.

This concentration of finance and power has led Yeouido to sometimes be referred to as the "Manhattan of Seoul," in keeping with the unfortunate national habit of making overstretched comparisons with Western locales (see: Jeju Island is the Hawaii of Korea; Seoul's Seorae Village is the Paris of Korea; Seoul National University is the Harvard of Korea). Forced metaphors aside, Yeouido does exude an air of Serious Business, and its status as the country's seat of economic power does at least mirror that of Gotham. Hit up the neighborhood around noon on a weekday and watch the sidewalks turn into rivers of power suits flowing between shiny skyscrapers covered in purple-, cobalt-, black-, or aquamarine-tinted glass.

Yeouido isn't all work and no play, however. Thanks to its combination of flatness, designated bike lanes, and wide sidewalks, the island is one of the best spots in the city for recreational cycling, and when you want to get off the pavement two impressive parks offer escapes from the glass and steel canyon.

Neatly bisecting the island where the airport's runway was once located, the lengthy Yeouido Park is divided into four distinct sections. At its center is Culture Plaza, a paved expanse dominated by an enormous Korean flag. Its edges are ringed with popular pickup basketball courts, and when I passed by there were also fathers playing catch with sons and a pair of old ladies sharing a tandem bike. As its name implies, the plaza also hosts events and concerts, and on the day I was there a group of workers was setting up a stage for some type of performance. While they worked, a monumental sound system blared out the same adult contemporary song over and over again, as if the city were adding sleep-deprivation resistance training to the public air raid drills it periodically holds, a precaution instigated by threats from the country's belligerent northern neighbor.

South of the plaza, the Nature and Ecology Forest was more peaceful, with a boardwalk looping through miniature versions

of a variety of eco-zones. On one stretch of the walk, I came across a photo shoot taking place, a not uncommon occurrence in the park. In a country where the selfie is an art form, the picturesque area is popular with both professional and amateur photographers.

On the other side of the plaza, the Jandi Madang, an open space of gently undulating knolls dotted with trees, is an ideal spot for a picnic in warm weather or for playing in the snow in winter. Like the Ecological Forest, there was a small pond here, overlooked by a country-style thatched roof pavilion.

The Traditional Korean Forest, at the far north end, was a simple, unflashy section where walking paths wound between the trees, all of which were species native to the peninsula. There was yet another pond there, at the divide between the forest and the field. It was probably the prettiest one in the park, and as I admired it I watched four ducks paddle around and occasionally plunge into the water in search of something to eat.

Meticulously groomed Yeouido Park's hippie sibling, Yeouido Saetgang Ecological Park forms the island's southwestern border, connecting with Hangang Park to create a green loop encircling the island. A *saetgang* refers to a small channel separating an island from a riverbank, and the park is a semi-marshy area that abuts one such channel. Although it's an engineered wetland, the park's sculpting is minimal and only feels artificial in a couple of spots. In a city where the truly natural is nearly impossible to come by, though, close enough is often also good enough. One of these artificial-feeling spots is near the park entrance, where a cascade tumbles into a pond. Above the pond is the wonderful Saetgang Bridge, a pedestrian crossing joining Yeouido to Seoul's south bank. Cables on this thin, curvaceous span link diagonal poles to the walkway, creating two triangular wings and giving the structure the look of a lithe metallic dragon.

Although not quite big enough to get lost in—the drone of traffic is always present (and often visible), and the tops of office and apartment towers hog the horizon—the park is still one of the most "natural" places that one can visit in Seoul. While there, I frequently found myself alone on the dirt paths, with nothing for company but the bent willow trees and the breeze rattling dried reeds like rainsticks.

Ultimately, though, Yeouido is about adventures in capitalism, and adventures, as adventures do, sometimes lead to strange places. After leaving the park, I walked past a Coffee Bean & Tea Leaf. Was there a car parked inside that Coffee Bean? Were there *four* cars parked inside? There were. And there were people reading at tables, just as natural as could be, completely indifferent to the fact that at the next table there wasn't actually a table. There was a car.

I looked up at the Coffee Bean sign. A Hyundai one was right next to it. Was this a café with a showroom in the middle of it? Or was it a showroom surrounded by a café? It was like looking at a corporate-sponsored version of Rubin's vase: container for flowers or two people facing each other? The questions in my mind didn't end there. I got the appeal of having a coffee while you looked at new cars, but why would you want to drink coffee surrounded by a bunch of mid-priced family-friendly sedans? Wouldn't that new car smell spoil the scent of coffee, and vice versa? Was there somewhere nearby I could sip on a Frappuccino while browsing whiteware? And, most pointedly, huh?

Key places: Yeouido Park, Yeouido Saetgang Ecological Park

SPIRITS OF THE PAST

*At Dongnimmun, the country's colonial and spiritual
history poke through its modern façade*

Seoul's modern history is a tumultuous one, but the city keeps
its scars hidden beneath hard-earned layers of development
and success. There are some places, though, where the wounds
have been left exposed, and to get a glimpse of the troubles the
capital has been through one would do well to pay a visit to
Dongnimmun.

The name of this neighborhood, northwest of the main royal
palace, means "Independence Gate." The eponymous arch that's
its primary landmark was constructed in 1897 and modeled after
France's Arc de Triomphe, as seemingly all arches everywhere are.
Previously, the spot had been the location of a different gate, Yeo-
ngeunmun Gate, where Korean representatives met envoys from
the suzerain Ming and Qing Dynasties, paying fealty and pre-

senting them with gifts. Soon after the First Sino-Japanese War ended, the gate was demolished, and a year later Dongnimmun Gate was completed. Nearby is a statue of Soh Jaipil, the independence activist responsible for organizing the gate's construction. The large gray stones of the archway frame Seodaemun Independence Park, inside of which is Seodaemun Prison History Hall. Its entryway, set in a redbrick wall, features a gambrel roof next to a gray octagonal watchtower. Paired together, the two looked uncannily like the barns and silos that dotted the landscape of my Wisconsin childhood, and for a moment I was taken back to those days, driving past rolling green hills and fields of sweet corn. Many of those drives also took me past the Columbia Correctional Institution, a maximum-security facility covering 27 acres of high-walled, concertina-wired buildings, all watched over by armed guards. It was the prison that had shaped my idea of prisons, and Seodaemun Prison, by comparison, looked quaint and unintimidating, though its appearance was no indication of what had once happened there.

Built in 1908, in the early stages of Japan's colonization of Korea, Seodaemun Prison was meant to hold 500 inmates. A mere 11 years later it held 3,000, an indication of both the vigor of the Korean resistance and the severity with which the Japanese repressed it. In the 1930s, the prison expanded to 30 times its original size of 1,600 square meters, growing to accommodate the explosion in arrests of Korean independence activists.

Once they arrived at Seodaemun, prisoners were confined to triple-bolted cells and forced to work in one of the prison's 12 factories, producing materials for the Japanese army, mostly textiles and clothing. Below the cells were interrogation and torture rooms. One form of torture used here consisted of a prisoner being strung up upside down while a guard poured water from a kettle up their nose to simulate drowning. They simply called it water torture. Today it's known as waterboarding, and in a biting irony the man who provided the U.S. government's legal rationale for its use during the Bush Administration, the lawyer John Yoo, was himself born in Seoul.

In a rather disorienting contrast with the deprivations and abuses that once occurred here, the actual grounds of the prison are beautiful. The stately redbrick buildings contrast with the bright-green grass, and the entire complex is surrounded by hills that are often shrouded in mist. The one edifice that scars the lovely scene is tucked away in the far southwest corner. The Execution Building is a homely structure of unpainted wood planks. Inside, three benches face what looks like a miniature stage, where a noose hangs above a stool set on a trap door. There are even curtains, and one wonders if they were opened for the performance or closed before the final act.

Seodaemun Prison is fronted by the rising peak of Mt. Inwangsan. Gazing up at it from the prison yard, I wondered if the presence of Seoul's most spiritual mountain just outside would have served as a source of comfort to the inmates, or of frustration, knowing it was there but being unable to reach it.

When I arrived at the mountain's entrance after leaving the prison I could hear the pounding of drums coming from above, and I followed their sound. As I climbed, the drums stopped, and off to the right I noticed a monk in gray robes and a wide-brimmed straw hat ascending some steps, big plastic bags of groceries in each hand. The moment he disappeared through a gate the drums took up their cadence again, this time joined by a pair of cymbals and a *piri*, a keening Korean flute. Soon I reached the source of the music: an old-fashioned wooden building painted in the familiar burgundy with emerald trim, its eaves finished off with bright and intricate detailing. Vivid robes hung from a thin rope across a doorway, and inside was a large altar stacked with fruit and flowers, all arranged around a pig's head, its mouth stuffed full of money. Several people in all-white traditional dress sat inside, two of them next to the open doorframe smoking cigarettes and blowing their smoke outside. An elderly woman dressed in splendid royal-blue robes and a red hat with two pheasant feathers sticking straight up closed her eyes and began to walk around rhythmically in front of the altar, bouncing slightly on the balls of her feet.

The woman was a *mudang*, a female shaman, and the building I was standing in front of was Guksadang, the country's most important shamanist shrine, said to house the spirit of King Taejo, founder of the Joseon Dynasty. Originally located on Mt. Namsan, it was rebuilt on Mt. Inwangsan after being demolished by the Japanese in 1925.

The Korean belief systems that predate Buddhism are animist and center on the natural world, mountains in particular. One of their most distinct features is *gut* (pronounced "goot"), rites performed to do everything from pray for a bountiful harvest to initiate a new shaman.

I had by chance arrived just as a *gut* was beginning, and I lingered outside for a bit, unsure whether I was welcome. Just as I was about to leave, one of the assistants, a woman with a small streak of hot pink in her hair, waved me around to the side and invited me in, and I sat down to watch the ceremony. This particular one was a memorial service. Attending were the deceased's widow, some sons and daughters, and a grandchild who seemed more interested in his ice cream than in what was going on around him. Indeed, as the *mudang* alternated between intoning, bouncing, walking about in front of the altar, and appealing to the spirits in a chant-talk before the family, the expressions on the sons' and daughters' faces were mostly ones of forbearance, indulging mom in a belief they themselves had lost or, more likely, never had.

As intrigued as I was by the *gut*, like the family members I also found it hard to reconcile the ceremony—its mysticism, chants, and trances—with the modern Seoul I knew. At one point the family was ushered outside, seated on the temple steps, and given a large sheet of paper to hold over their heads. The shaman sprinkled it first with water, then a mixture of sesame seeds, eggs, and bean paste. She waved flags above the mourners' heads and banged a pair of knives together before stabbing the air with them. Finally, she took the paper, lit it on fire, and waved it around before taking a sip of liquid and spitting it in a spray over the family's heads. How much of *guts* and traditional shamanism was true belief, I wondered, and how much was the simple stubborn insistence on maintaining something ancient and purely Korean as a rebuke to the modern, globalized world?

After the performance on the steps, the *gut* reached a point where it began to turn into a session of genuine mourning, and I quietly took my leave. I hiked a short ways up to Seonbawi, the Zen Rocks, so called because of their alleged resemblance to a pair of robed monks absorbed in meditation, though my secular mind was unable to make out anything even remotely monk-like in their appearance. What they mostly looked like to me were giant chunks of half-melted butter that someone had taken swipes out of with their fingers, or an ooze creature that had risen up from the ground only to glimpse Medusa. Dozens of pigeons perched acrobatically on the rocks, many of them cocked at odd angles, and with no more drums sounding from below, their cooing was the only noise filling the air. From the base of the rocks, an unhindered view revealed Seodaemun Prison, Jongno Tower, and the hundreds of high-rises that have sprung up in the decades since independence. Beyond those were the mountains that ring Seoul on all sides, forms that have been there since before this place became a city and that will be there after everything else has passed.

Key places: Dongnimmun Gate, Seodaemun Independence Park, Seodaemun Prison History Hall, Mt. Inwangsan, Guksadang, Seonbawi

LUSH LIFE

Oases amid the urban jungle

What struck me about Bangi was the color. Seoul's canvas is mostly a palette of grays, metals, burgundies, and less-than-whites. But in Bangi, everywhere I looked there was green. Streets were lined with trees, medians were rich with ground cover, and walls were latticed with ivy. It seemed as if I were in a completely different city.

Everyone in Seoul who isn't an employee of a concrete company has lamented the city's lack of green space—the combined result of the decades-long population boom that began after the Korean War, the pressing need to house all the new arrivals, and the country's single-minded focus on development throughout the latter half of the 20th century. These circumstances led to a "build first, ask questions later" mentality that has only recently given way to a more measured examination of what the city should be and what kind of life it should provide for its residents. But considering the huge challenge of establishing more parkland in one of the most densely populated metropolises in the world, the progress the city has made in this regard over the past decade is encouraging, and neighborhoods like Bangi hint at how the capital is slowly becoming a more verdant, more livable city.

So how does this happen in a place where open space can at times seem as elusive as the Higgs boson? One way is by mimicking a circulatory system, emphasizing not large expanses but arteries that wind through preexisting developments. Just south of Bangi Station was a space about 10 meters wide, tucked between the multilaned Yangjae-daero and an apartment complex and given the awkward English name of The Best View Point. Within that strip were a man-made, rock-lined brooklet and a small embankment lush with shrubs, wildflowers, and long grasses. Two rows of trees shaded a walking path where the sound of the passing traffic may not have been blocked, but the view of it almost was. It wasn't very big, but by making strategic use of the space available, The Best View Point transformed what would have been just another brutally exposed stretch of pavement into something rather lovely.

I walked the length of the path, blood pressure lowered, all the way to Ogeum-ro before swinging a right and arriving at the Bangi-dong ancient Baekje-era tombs. Located well outside the city walls hundreds of years ago, modern development saw these and other burial grounds swallowed up by the city, and the need to preserve them led to a second, almost accidental, way of carving oases out of the surrounding urban expanse. Stepping through the entrance, I was met by a grassy lawn dotted with trees that separated eight reconstructed tumuli into two equal groups. Four green domes occupied a hill in the northwest corner. The grass on three was neatly trimmed, but the fourth tumulus was a bit wilder and had a blue tarp weighed down with rocks and piles of dirt running over it like an inverted Mohawk. I peered through some metal bars, and at the end of a low stone passageway into the tomb I could just make out a slightly larger area where a collection of stones created a rough bed.

The tumuli in the park each consisted of a square or rectangular chamber on top of a stone base, and the interiors of some had vaulted ceilings and coffin platforms, like the one in the gloom of that first burial mound. The tombs here had been raided long before their discovery in 1975, but some blue-gray stoneware dishes and jars were recovered at that time. The stoneware was thought to date to the Baekje period (18 BCE–660 CE), hence the name given to the site, but it's now believed that the tombs themselves are slightly more recent constructions, dating to the Unified Silla period (676–935).

A path between the tombs led to the top of a hill, from where I could see a ridge of forested mountains away in the distance to the southeast, like uncut versions of the swells gently rising and falling below me. There were four more tombs on the opposite side of the park, and those too were ringed by a dirt track. Judging by the footwear choices and determined expressions on the faces of the women who were my companions on the path, I was the only one who'd come for the history. Everyone else was there for the exercise.

Leaving the tombs, I walked a short ways to nearby Olympic Park. Built for the 1988 Summer Games, it was one of the modern city's first instances of channeling its eagerness to build into the construction of a large-scale green space—a blueprint that would later be used to create Seoul Forest, the Hangang Parks, and the sprawling World Cup Park. In the complex's southeast corner was Rose Plaza, set in front of the big white bubble that is the tennis stadium. The flowers were a bit battered from the previous day's heavy rain, but a number of families and couples were still out admiring them, helped by the useful boards listing the names of the different species. There were roses of every hue, but the most eye-catching thing in the plaza was "A Virtual Sphere," a huge orb of red-and-blue hanging tubes that resembled the *taegeuk* design in the center of the South Korean flag.

Just west of Rose Plaza and opposite the Olympic Convention Center I found Wildflower Hill. A dirt path ran around a small field of grasses and red wildflowers, and I followed it first to a small pavilion at the top of the rise, and then down the other side, where the flowers came in more varied hues: reds, blues, pinks, and lavenders. It was quieter, more secluded, and altogether prettier than the plaza, but with only a fraction of the people. A thick screen of trees separated it from the adjacent road, and I could almost, *almost*, trick myself into thinking I was in a country meadow. In a neighborhood of uncommon lushness, this felt like the most idyllic, most romantic spot of all. Lovers, this one's for you.

Key places: The Best View Point (Nambusunhwan-ro), Bangi-dong ancient Baekje-era tombs, Olympic Park, Rose Plaza, Wildflower Hill

HAVEN'T WE MET BEFORE?

Welcome to my home. It's just like your home. Please come in.

Banpo is the sort of place that, unless you lived there, you'd have no reason to go there. There is, to put it bluntly, nothing of interest to the non-resident. Look south across Sinbanpo-ro and apartment complexes are all you'll see. Look east and west and it's the same. North of the station, more apartments. The immediate impression is that it's a bit soulless and proof of an oft-heard criticism of Seoul: that one neighborhood looks just like the next, a repeating loop of indistinguishable apartment towers and chain stores. It's a criticism leveled as often by Seoulites as by outsiders.

If you take a closer look at the city's urban fabric, however, you discover that this isn't the case and that the city, in fact, possesses an inconspicuous diversity to its neighborhoods. Nevertheless, certain places do embody that vision of Seoul as a copy-and-paste expanse of endlessly reproduced apartment blocks, and Banpo is one of them.

Many people (and again this applies to Koreans as much as non-Koreans) are apt to look at Gangnam, in which Banpo is situated, as the factory engine of the country's econo-beauty complex, a place where social pressures and the expectations of others lead to people being shunted through the cram school–plastic surgery–conglomerate production line, resulting in a place where a great many individuals come out respectably employed, respectably housed, respectably indistinguishable, and respectably uninteresting.

Banpo, I felt, was a pretty good example of the type of residential area that process results in, and when the major things breaking up the apartment blocks were a strip mall and a shopping center, the neighborhood didn't put up much of an argument. It was, frankly, a bit dispiriting, and if Seoul truly was dominated by neighborhoods as mundane as this, for many it would be a terribly tedious place to live.

It should be remembered, though, that for others that mundaneness is utterly agreeable. In Banpo, the streets are calm and tree-lined, and the buzz of cicadas is the principal sound in summer. The parents pushing babies in expensive strollers seem genuinely happy. The kids running around on their own carefree, the people in cafés and loading groceries into cars perfectly content. It's fair to reproach a culture that at times wrings individuality and a sense of adventure out of people, but to bemoan a community like Banpo is a bit disingenuous. These types of neighborhoods may be a product of that culture, but in a megacity with severely limited space, apartment block farms are a necessity and, in the full-speed-ahead way that Seoul had to develop after the war, to some extent unavoidable. Nor is this type of neighborhood unique to Korea. After all, even in America, where individuality is a religion, the suburbs and exurbs that so many people live in are often lamented as theaters of nothing, filled with bland prefab houses and big box stores. One way to look at the symmetry of identical latches on identical windows on identical apartments on identical towers is to see banal conformity; another is to admit that sometimes all we want is to find a simple place where we can take comfort in not being a stranger.

WRITERS' RETREAT

Visions of the literary life in Seongbuk-dong

Koreans have a term for autumn they sometimes use; they call it the season of reading, and it's at this time of year that I most like to go to the Seongbuk-dong neighborhood. The air there seems a bit fresher, the pace a bit slower. There's history, too, mostly not of the grand, Story of the Nation variety but of simple, dignified lives, often lived with a literary devotion. Altogether, it feels like an escape from the city and its ills: its traffic, its impatience, its overstimulation—a village apart.

There's much to see and do in the area, usually too much for one visit alone, but if I could combine all of my favorite spots into one trip, this is how I'd do it. I'd begin at the neighborhood's most recognizable landmark, Hyehwamun Gate, one of the four minor gates in the old city walls. Hyehwamun was originally built in 1397 but was demolished during the Japanese colonial period to make way for a tramline. The year 1992 finally saw the gate's reconstruction, slightly north of the original location, and today the old wall's northeast gate sits impressively on a rise overlooking the road, its emerald-green trim jumping out from the gray stones forming both its base and the city wall running north.

From near the gate, I'd hop on one of the neighborhood buses that trundle north toward Mt. Bugaksan and into Seongbuk-dong. The first place I'd go would be the Choi Sunu House, the old residence of the art historian and former director general of the National Museum of Korea. Dating to the 1930s, it's a lovely home built in the traditional style: laid out in the shape of the Korean character ㄴ and capped by black roof tiles over sturdy wood beams. One wing displays some of Choi's personal belongings in a glass case—pipe, camera, glasses, medals he was awarded—while the other wing shows how it existed as his home: a sleeping mat in a corner, a bookshelf, some low tables with dishes and paintbrushes. In a rear courtyard, young bamboo shoots sprout up. The house is not far from the neighborhood's main street, and I can usually hear the murmur of motorbikes and the small trucks blaring scratchy recorded pitches for vegetables, but they do little to break the tranquility.

From the Choi Sunu House, I'd cross back over Seongbuk-dong-gil and turn right on Seonjam-ro. On the corner is the site of the Seonjamdan Altar, built in 1473 to honor the goddess of silkworms. This is where the Joseon royalty prayed for good years of silkworm farming and made sacrifices to Seonjam, a figure also known by her Chinese name, Xi Lingshi. I'd follow alongside the long altar grounds, parallel to the road, then continue until the street ended at the gate to Seongnagwon. This traditional garden, originally a villa for a Joseon official and then a detached palace, is supposedly one of the most beautiful places in Seoul. I say "supposedly" because the garden is privately owned and operated and, despite receiving up to KRW 1.5 billion (USD 1.3 million) in public funding to maintain the grounds, its owners have refused to open it to the public.

Rather than taking Seonjam-ro to Seongnagwon, I might instead head down Seongbuk-ro 16-gil to arrive via the backstreets. This route would take me past a small granite plaque denoting where the home of renowned poet Jo Ji-hun once stood, just one of the unexpected surprises that tend to turn up in this neighborhood, a place where galleries and hat shops sit alongside recycling yards. Now a four-story apartment building sits on the plot, and out front there's a concrete bench where residents might play *janggi*, or Korean chess. Near the garden I might also pass, as I once did, a family just sitting in their parked car, windows down, enjoying the weather. The mom, in the passenger seat, had taken her shoes off and propped her bare feet up on the dash. The neighborhood's kind of like that.

If the garden was still closed I could take a fork to the right that leads to the Diplomatic Village, an area where many ambassadors have their official residences, including those from China, Afghanistan, and Papua New Guinea. Signs pointing to the Australian ambassador's enormous house show just a kangaroo and an arrow. Quiet roads twist between impressive walled homes, the occasional Mercedes or Lexus drives past, and seemingly every building has a sign on it notifying passersby that it's protected by the local SECOM Security firm. If the area weren't so hilly it would be excellent for walking; the only sound you consistently hear is birdsong, and it can be entertaining to pick out the different ambassadors' residences—celebrity house sighting for wonks.

After meandering up and down the quiet roads of the Diplomatic Village, I'd return past Seongnagwon and turn back onto Seonjam-ro. A long walk down the road, lined on either side with brick or stone walls, would lead me to the elaborately painted wooden gate marking the entrance to the beautiful Buddhist sanctuary of Gilsangsa Temple. A library and an elegant main hall housing a gilt, slightly less than life-sized Buddha occupy the front of the complex, but the further back one goes the more peaceful and otherworldly the complex becomes. Sitting in a forest valley, the temple's paths, stairs, and buildings follow the land's natural contours, and the entire complex is surrounded by trees, shrubs, and bamboo. A tiny mountain stream babbles down one of the slopes.

Gilsangsa's setting makes it feel ancient—it's easy to think you've stepped onto the set of a Chinese kung fu epic and that at any moment warrior monks will come whooshing through the treetops—but in fact it's one of Seoul's youngest temples, opened in 1997. It also has one of the most curious origin stories. Before becoming Gilsangsa Temple, the complex on the slope of Mt. Samgaksan was Daewongak, one of Korea's most exclusive restaurants and a renowned *gisaeng* house. *Gisaeng*, like Japanese geishas, were female courtesans trained in dance, music, and poetry, and Daewongak's owner, Kim Yeong-han, was herself a former *gisaeng*. At the same time that Kim was building and overseeing Daewongak and its precursor, a middle-aged monk from the southern tip of the peninsula named Beopjeong was rapidly gaining a following for his writings on the simple, examined life. At some point, Kim came across his most famous work, the essay *Musoyu* (Non-possession). After reading it she found the monk and asked him to take Daewongak and turn it into a temple. Following 10 years of persuading, Beopjeong finally relented. The restaurant was valued at nearly KRW 100 billion (USD 90 million).

Once I'd left the temple I'd return to Seongbuk-dong-gil and climb up a set of concrete steps that begin their ascent just a few paces down an easy-to-miss alley. I'd pass several rough-looking tin-roofed homes before coming to a gate marked with a stone plaque and Chinese characters. This is Simujang, the former residence of "Manhae" Han Yong-un—poet, monk, independence activist, and one of the 33 national representatives of Korea's March 1, 1919, independence movement. Most *hanok* face south to capture as much sunlight as possible, but Simujang faces north, a symbolic decision Han took in order to turn his back, so to speak, on the Government-General building, the hub of Japanese colonial power. It wasn't a bad decision aesthetically speaking, either, as the austere three-room home takes in lovely views of the hills to the northeast.

Finally, to end my visit, I'd go to Suyeon Sanbang. The former home of novelist Yi Tae-jun, Suyeon Sanbang's conversion into a teahouse was done with a minimal amount of disturbance to what the building once was, perhaps unsurprising since the conversion was undertaken by Yi's granddaughter. Old books rest in glass cases, an antique phone and Singer sewing machine sit nearby, and a black-and-white family portrait—Yi surrounded by his wife and five kids—hangs on the wall. Several low tables are set up inside the house, with a couple more on the lawn out front, and menus are printed on *hanji*, a traditional Korean paper made from mulberry pulp. I'd sit down and order a cold-plum tea and begin to entertain thoughts of doing as Choi, Jo, Beopjeong, Manhae, and Yi did. Of quitting my job, canceling my phone contract, and giving away whatever I didn't need. Of leaving behind the trappings of the rest of Seoul and moving to Seongbuk-dong. Of finding a simple *hanok* with just enough room for a bed, some bookshelves, and a sturdy desk and chair.

Of sitting down and writing.

Key places: Hyehwamun Gate, Seongbuk-dong, Choi Sunu House, Seonjamdan Altar, Seongnagwon, Diplomatic Village, Gilsangsa Temple, Simujang, Old Yi Tae-jun House (Suyeon Sanbang)

ILLUMINATION

Among the lanterns

It's the most wonderful time of the year in Seoul—the beginning of the fourth lunar month, when the city holds its Lotus Lantern Festival to celebrate the birth of the Buddha. There's an oft-absent gladness in the air, and everywhere you look, innumerable paper lanterns are strung up along the streets, giving the capital the cheerful appearance of having been invaded by incandescent gumdrops.

Although Buddhism has been replaced by Christianity as the country's most followed religion, the faith's long history here has strongly influenced the culture, and lantern festivals can be traced back as far as the Silla Kingdom (57 BCE–935 CE). The earliest reference to one is found in the *Samguksagi*, a historical record of three early Korean kingdoms, which dates back to 866.

Officially sanctioned lotus lantern festivals were held during the Goryeo Dynasty (918–1392) before being banned in the Confucian Joseon era (1392–1910), but many local communities kept the tradition alive through informal celebrations. Buddha's birthday was made a national holiday in 1975, and for the past two decades the Lotus Lantern Parade has wound its way through downtown Seoul, the current route going from Dongdaemun to Jogyesa Temple.

By late afternoon on the day of the parade, the street festival that had been taking place on Wujeongguk-ro, the street between Jonggak Station and Jogyesa Temple, was beginning to wrap up. Both sides of the road were lined with half-disassembled tents as workers hurried to clear the way for the procession's final leg. Hundreds of tourists were walking about, most moving in the opposite direction I was, toward Jongno to stake out a spot for the parade. Weaving their way through the visitors were files of police, locals in various old-fashioned costumes, and children in *hanbok*, or traditional Korean clothing.

Many of the businesses along Wujeongguk-ro are Buddhist supply stores and monastic clothing shops catering to the area's monks and devotees, and the street reminded me of Rome's Via dei Cestari, where the city's Catholic clergy goes for its albs and thuribles. And just as I had done on that little cobblestoned strip south of the Pantheon, I was now having the same amused realization all over again—that these men and women of the cloth . . . well, they too had to actually buy that cloth somewhere.

Besides robes, the shops on the road to Jogyesa Temple sell everything from tiny lotus votive candles, mini-pagoda statuettes, and prayer beads to incense burners and Buddha figures of all shapes and sizes. Naturally, there were also myriad paper lanterns for the holiday season, even ones shaped like cartoon characters.

My favorite sight, though, was a shop window where three gray robes hung in front of bright red and gold pillows, creating a tableau like mountains in autumn.

I soon joined the drift of tourists and locals heading back to Jongno to settle in for the parade. While waiting for the light at the corner, I found myself standing amid a group of *pungmul* musicians, who were dressed in bright costumes and hats that looked something like nuns' cornettes with gumballs stuck atop them. *Pungmul* is a traditional style of music heavily associated with rural communities and collective farming, and on any other day seeing a troupe waiting patiently on a traffic island, instruments on their hips, the shadows of skyscrapers stretched across them, would be like spotting a band of minstrels on Fifth Avenue. On that evening, however, it all seemed very normal. Then the light changed and we all crossed the street.

On the other side of the road was a structure that has a tendency to disappear a bit among the surrounding high-rises, despite being one of the most historically significant in Seoul (if not for the actual current structure, at least for the heritage it represents). Bosingak Pavilion was built in 1979 and the bell it houses cast in 1985, but their lineage can be traced back to 1395, when the original belfry was built and the bell inside was used to mark the opening and closing of the city gates. For the night of the parade, however, Bosingak Pavilion was merely serving as the backdrop for an enormous stage where musical performances were being held.

Finally, as dusk fell, the procession began. Thousands of Buddhist monks, nuns, and laypeople marched down the avenue, each carrying a one-meter pole, at the end of which bobbed a glowing paper lantern. Interspersed with the marchers were huge, luminous floats of the infant Buddha in his one-finger-raised "I got it" pose or of mechanized dragons, their legs rotating, heads swiveling from side to side. I don't know that I've ever seen as many smiling Koreans all in one place as I did at the lantern parade. The route from Dongdaemun to Jogyesa is no short walk, but even near the end the marchers were ebullient, waving to onlookers and occasionally slipping out of formation to unhook their lantern and hand it to an excited kid. The entire affair was a bewitching sight, its charm amplified by Korea's dearth of holidays and the country's often strained relationship with the pursuit of joy.

With the parade nearly completed, I left my seat and followed the marchers toward Jogyesa Temple. The entire temple courtyard was canopied in rows of blue, white, yellow, red, orange, pink, and green lanterns that formed a Korean yin-yang in the center, nearly blocking out the sky above. Standing underneath it was like standing inside of a giant prism. The smaller courtyard fronting Great Hero Hall was also covered with hanging lanterns, and while devotees made their way up to them, the three giant gilded Buddhas inside the hall looked out onto the courtyard's enormous 500-year-old Chinese Scholar Tree. Its top disappeared into the nimbus of lanterns overhead, as if its branches might reach all the way to heaven.

As I left Jogyesa Temple I passed under One Pillar Gate, which separates the complex from the city outside. Because this was Korea, and it's practically law that some sort of diversionary technology must exist everywhere, an interactive digital image of a koi pond, complete with virtual lily pads, was projected on the ground underneath the gate. It says a great deal about the country that the only two places I've ever seen this were inside COEX, the largest underground mall in Asia, and here, at Korea's main temple of Zen Buddhism. The fish lazily "swam" about, but would quickly scatter if someone stepped too near them. After startling the digital kois with my careless feet, I headed past several parked but still glowing floats back to Jongno. There, the crowds had still not scattered, not willing to let go of Seoul's most magical night just yet.

Key places: Bosingak, Buddhist supply stores and monastic clothing shops, Jogyesa Temple

EX-RESIDENTS

Returning to the neighborhood I never knew

In the 1960s and '70s, as the city's modernization shifted into high gear, large numbers of residents living in the Hannam-dong neighborhood and around the Cheonggyecheon Stream in central Seoul were relocated to make way for development projects. Overwhelmingly poor, some simply living as squatters, many of them were resettled in Sanggye-dong, in the far northeast, where roughly 1,500 small homes had been built with government assistance. Surrounded by mountains on three sides, the area was largely cut off from the rest of the city and devoid of public transport connecting it to the major markets, still vital nexuses of commerce at the time. The government promised that this would be the residents' final relocation and encouraged them to put down roots.

Then, in 1981, Seoul was named the host city for the 1988 Summer Olympics. Despite being nowhere near the main Olympic venues, Sanggye-dong was considered an eyesore and became the target of further urban renewal efforts by the government. In 1986, the subway system was extended, connecting the neighborhood to the rest of Seoul. Soon after, the residents of Sanggye-dong were told that they would be relocated yet again so that high-rise apartments could be constructed for the middle class. The locals would be given a roughly KRW 1 million resettlement fee per family and sent to Pocheon, a village about 30 kilometers from the Demilitarized Zone.

Needless to say, many of the residents felt this was unacceptable, but there was little they could do to stop the bulldozers from moving in. Though many families saw no other option than to reluctantly pack their bags, others refused, and a tent city quickly sprang up. Intermittent protests arose, culminating in a June 1986 showdown between about 1,000 residents and an equal number of police and government-hired thugs. By the end of the day, one of the protesters was dead.

Ultimately, the protesting residents were forced out. Many of them relocated to Bucheon, a satellite city west of Seoul, where together they purchased a plot of land abutting the highway. Two years later, a runner would pass by that spot carrying the Olympic Torch on its final stretch from Incheon to the Olympic Stadium. Everything the runner wore—tank top, jogging shorts, socks, shoes, gloves, sweatband—was pristine white, and draped around his neck was a huge garland of flowers. Surrounding him were police motorcycles and television crews, and following behind was a float in the shape of a dragon, ridden by beautiful women in blue-and-yellow traditional gowns. As the runner made the slow ceremonial jog, he beamed and waved at the cheering onlookers assembled at the edges of the highway. The ex-residents of Sanggye-dong were not in the crowd that day. The City of Bucheon had deemed their makeshift buildings too unseemly for the procession route and had torn them down, forcing their owners to take temporary shelter in underground tunnels they'd dug.

All of this was only 30 years ago, but that's a lifetime in terms of what happens in Seoul, and one could be forgiven for being shocked by these abuses, for forgetting that the country was barely a democracy at the time, or for being totally unaware that this ever happened at all. I'll be the first to ask for pardon. From 2009 to 2010 I lived in Junggye-dong, right next to Sanggye, yet knew nothing of the area's history until after I left. Though I lived in the area for a year, I never explored or got to know it well, as the neighborhood didn't seem to merit much exploring. So when I returned a year later I was curious to answer the question of what I'd overlooked.

In the area north of the station, it seemed I'd missed very little. It wasn't hard, in fact, to imagine that the Sanggye area had no history, so squarely did it fit into the model image of modern middle-class Seoul, which I suppose was what the government had in mind all along. Epitomizing outer-Seoul living, it was a mix of apartment towers, small businesses, and chain stores, and in the backstreets it could be so quiet that at various times the loudest sounds were spinning barber poles and someone in a house sharpening knives. To the east rose Mt. Buramsan's handsome deep-green and tan peak.

South of the station was the Danghyeoncheon, a stream with two very different sides. Its source was a big rusty industrial pipe in the side of a wall, with water spilling onto a wide, algae-dotted slab of concrete before tumbling into what was basically a gash in the floor, as if a tremor had cracked the paving open. The walls underneath a nearby pedestrian bridge were covered in graffiti—there were pictures of Eazy-E, Homer Simpson, and SpongeBob SquarePants, and another scrawl reading "Notorious P.I.G." Just on the other side of that bridge, though, the Danghyeoncheon Stream was as nice as any stream you'd find in the city—manicured and engineered, with carefully placed rocks on the embankments, small sandbars, and colorful wildflowers. A handful of ducks lazily drifted with the current until someone's pet terrier bounded into the water after them, chasing the birds downstream.

Crossing to the stream's south bank, I came upon a pair of small monuments. One was a statue titled *Carved at Heart*, a tribute to Yi Mun-geon, who, in nearby Hagye-dong, had made the first tombstone carving in Hangeul, the Korean script. The other was an engraving of the poem "The Bird" by the poet Cheon Sang-byeong. They were tributes to Korea's progress and beauty, in a setting that demonstrated both. Nowhere, however, was there a monument to the old residents of Sanggye-dong.

Key place: Danghyeoncheon Stream

WAITING

For lunch, for the wrecking ball, for a king in exile

If it's true that the way to a man's heart is through his stomach, then this must be as true of where a man gets his food as it is of who cooks it, which may help explain my unexpected affinity for the Changsin neighborhood.

What keeps me coming back is a little two-story joint called Naksan Naengmyeon, which I came upon the way that so many favorite restaurants come to us: by accident. I had turned onto a side street at random, and about 20 meters down, a line of people curled out the door of a restaurant, despite the fact that it was 2:30, usually the start of the midafternoon lull. Obviously, I had to eat there.

Originating in what's now North Korea, *naengmyeon* is a dish of cold noodles that's especially popular in the summer or

as a chaser to greasy grilled meats. It's typically served in one of two styles: in a cold water broth as *mul-naengmyeon*, or as *bibim-naengmyeon*, with less water and more hot pepper sauce. Purists might scoff at Naksan's house *naengmyeon*, as it's neither true *mul* nor true *bibim-naengmyeon* but something in between, and the cucumber slivers, radish slices, and sesame seeds that garnish the dish, usually added with some restraint, are fairly shoveled on here, but purity is for horse breeders and nuns. The house *naengmeyon* is the only thing Naksan serves, and the only option you have when ordering is how spicy you want it, from spiceless through three increasing levels of heat according to how much chili paste is added. Many expats in Seoul (myself included) are frequently annoyed by Koreans' patronizing concerns that their food is too spicy, unaware that a lot of Westerners grew up in multicultural places eating Mexican, Indian, Thai, and other cuisines that are often hotter than your typical Korean dish. So it's also to Naksan Naengmyeon's great credit that it's the only restaurant I've ever been to in Korea where the old woman taking orders told me that I should probably go one hotter. In any case, if it turned out to be too hot I could always do as the large sign on the wall said: *If the* naengmyeon *seasoning isn't right (tart, sweet, spicy, salty) just yell "Auntie!"*

It may be the *naengmyeon* that keeps me coming back, but it's Changsin's uncanny way of revealing unexpected surprises while keeping other mysteries to herself that's made this one of my favorite places in Seoul to explore.

Part of the area's inscrutability can be attributed to its geography. The neighborhood is cut off on three sides—by Dongmangbong Peak to the north and by a pair of massive, nearly vertical gray-brown rock faces to the east and west—turning it into a cul-de-sac, a neighborhood sequestered from the rest of the city.

Many of the alleys that run off of the main street are tiny; in some places one can practically touch both walls with one's elbows. While considerable development has taken place to the south, the backstreets are still untouched, snugly filled with lovely if run-down old homes with solid wooden doors. Whenever I visit, nearly all of the faces I see on the backstreets are old ones, and I always wonder how long they've lived there and how long they'll be able to before the encroaching gentrification prices them out.

The last time I walked through those alleys, I also kept noticing large trash bags stuffed full of scraps of fabric, like psychedelic bubblegum bubbles. There were small sewing workshops too, including one where a hula hoop hung on the wall above long tables strewn with bolts of fabric. I thought that maybe those small workshops supplied the nearby Dongdaemun clothing markets, but when a Korean friend and I tried to find out, the man inside the only shop where someone was working shooed us away, saying he was too busy to talk.

North of the station, a long flight of stairs led up Dongmangbong Peak, and at the top a large gray metal wall rose up, the tips of a pair of cranes poking up behind it. The construction site was quiet on a Sunday, but peering through a gap in the fence I could see a former hillside that for the time being was just an enormous pit, with no sign of the apartments that would eventually go in.

It was startling, and yet utterly expected. Two years earlier I had stood in that same spot, and where now there was only a hole in the earth, then there had been a large community of old brick houses. They were nearly identical to those near the station below but with one major difference: Each one had been abandoned, tagged with a sign that it was marked for redevelopment and would be torn down. Coming up onto a small rise in one of the up-and-down alleyways, I'd been able to see all the way across the valley. The whole stretch was filled with empty structures, each bearing the same sign like a white flag—an entire neighborhood of dead homes. With lovely views of Mt. Bukhansan in the distance, it was easy to see why that was valuable real estate, and why those low-income residences would be torn down so that a developer could build yet another expensive apartment complex in their place. It wasn't clear how long the houses had been abandoned, but it had been long enough for nature to have already begun reestablishing itself. Enormous spider webs clung everywhere, one particularly large one hosting a colony of 50 gold-and-black spiders of varying sizes.

Knowing that the buildings were just going to be torn down and pounded into rubble, many of the ex-residents had chosen to simply leave behind unwanted possessions, and by peeking through cracks and broken windows, or by stepping through the occasional door that had been left open, it was possible to get a glimpse of the lives that used to be lived there: a bookshelf, a bicycle, a dish rack, pillows and blankets, a *Dora the Explorer* videotape. I'd seen no one else around and had thought that every house was empty, but just before heading back out to the street I spotted an elderly woman coming out of one of the homes. When she walked down its front steps my view of her was blocked by a wall; I couldn't tell if she was packing up some final possessions, scavenging for things left behind, or if she was holding out till the bitter end.

Not everything in Changsin is so impermanent, though. The neighborhood is also home to some quietly hiding historical sites.

Tucked in a shady nook west of the station, between apartments and a small Buddhist temple, was a concrete building that had been painted brown, with wood and paper doors and a wood-beam roof covered in thatch. It was a re-creation of Biudang House, the modest home of Yu Gwan, a scholar and high-ranking official in the Joseon government. Though a member of the aristocratic elite, Yu was notoriously frugal; the home's name can be translated to mean "a house that barely provides shelter from the rain," and a legend states that the structure was so humble that, when it rained, Yu would use an umbrella indoors, wondering how those people who weren't fortunate enough to have an umbrella in their homes were managing. Yu was also the ancestor of Yi Su-gwang, a diplomat and the author of the first Korean encyclopedia. Yi spent his childhood and later years in the house and, after achieving success as a scholar in his own right, chose "Biudang" as his *ho*, similar to a pen name for Joseon scholars, but with added meaning—a *ho* was also meant to reflect its owner's personal philosophy.

Behind Biudang House was a small half circle of stones with a circular carving in the rock above it: Jajudongsaem Well, where the deposed Queen Jeongsun washed clothes and made a living dyeing fabric. Likely due to iron in the water, clothes washed here would turn purple (*jaju*), which a plaque on the site informed visitors was a "sad" story. As someone who's mixed reds and whites in his laundry before, I can sympathize, but I'm not sure that quite qualifies as sad. What is sad is how the queen came to be a washerwoman.

In 1452, after succeeding his father, King Munjong, at the age of 12, Queen Jeongsun's husband, King Danjong, became the sixth king of the Joseon Dynasty. The kid, short on muscle, was soon overthrown by his uncle, Yi Yu, and exiled to Yeongwol in Gangwon-do province. Four years later, concerned about plots to return Danjong to the throne and displaying a ruthless amount of caution, Yi, now King Sejo, had the 16-year-old poisoned.

When he was usurped and exiled, King Danjong's young wife was thrown out of the palace and went to live at Jeongeobwon, on what is now Naksan-gil, just east of Changsin Station. There she waited for her husband, and, after his murder, spent her days in mourning until her own death in 1521. Although Jeongeobwon was where she lived, when Queen Jeongsun wished to gaze in the direction of Yeongwol and her departed king, she would walk north and climb the nearby Dongmangbong Peak, the same peak where, half a millennium later, an entire neighborhood would disappear.

Key places: Naksan Naengmyeon, Biudang House and Jajudongsaem Well, Jeongeobwon

EXIT PLANET SEOUL

Getting away or disappearing or something in between

Just outside Exits 3 and 4 at Gangbyeon Station, there were signs of people on the move. A half dozen food stalls lined the sidewalk, pouring steam into the winter air. In front of them, smokers worked their way through cigarettes, shoulders hunched against the cold, free hands clutching suitcase handles. After stubbing out the ends they turned and headed into the massive white building behind them, the East Seoul Bus Terminal, and a few minutes later they were off, away from the city for a weekend, or perhaps for good.

The travelers were primarily heading north or east, but buses from East Seoul Terminal carry passengers to every one of Korea's mainland provinces. Whether the plan is to hit the beach at Sokcho, hike Mt. Jirisan, or simply escape to someplace that isn't Seoul, you can get there from here.

Inside, ticket windows flanked a central lobby where crowds of people came and went: 20-somethings carrying snowboard bags; monks swaddled in gray robes, matching sacks slung from their shoulders; solo travelers with large suitcases and faraway expressions, their thoughts already somewhere else. A shoe shiner had set himself up on a bench underneath the central escalators and was busy polishing away at the black ankle boots of the middle-aged woman seated in front of him, while further in the back a couple dozen travelers sat on rows of yellow plastic chairs and watched a replay of a soccer game on TV.

Other people drifted down the wings extending from the main lobby to browse the stores selling last-minute travel needs: pharmacies, newspaper stands, shops for bags and clothes, convenience stores. The last of these were confined to cramped little storefronts, yet somehow still had to orient all of their products to catch the gazes of the people walking by. The result was merchandise packed together so tightly that the shelves disappeared— bags of chips and boxes of cookies stacked on and next to rice cakes and oranges, with dried squid and squirt guns and toy microphones hanging in front—an arrangement so intricate and compact it seemed that removing one item from the structure would cause the entire shop to collapse.

Past the convenience stores and under the dim lighting at the far end of each wing were banks of rusty old pay phones. In a country with a 100 percent rate of cell phone ownership and more mobile phones than people, they seemed like an anachronism, but a central aspect of Korean society keeps them stubbornly relevant, at least for one demographic. All able-bodied Korean males serve a mandatory 21-month stint in the military, and while on base they're not permitted to have a phone, which means that your average army grunt has to keep a pocket's worth of coins on him in case he needs to arrange a pick-up with his family or girlfriend when on leave. At the terminal I watched one such private, just off the bus, bags jammed onto the ledge in front of him, plugging coins into one of the phones, dialing and redialing until finally getting through on the fifth try.

For those who are staying in town and aren't enlisted, all of one's technological wishes, cell phone or otherwise, can be fulfilled across the street at Techno Mart. A central, glass-enclosed elevator takes visitors past floors of TVs, ovens, massaging chairs, and, in case you're feeling particularly sadistic, slide projectors. On the top floor is the movie theater that was Korea's first multiplex, a fact that surprised me because not only would I have expected the first one to have opened somewhere closer to downtown, but also because, in a city where it's difficult to *not* be looking at a screen at any given moment, it didn't open until 1998. While waiting for a movie to start, visitors can have their fortunes told by tarot card readers at one of five tables in the lobby, but, then again, knowing the ending takes all the fun out of things.

Not much interested in electronics, I pushed through a set of glass doors and stepped out onto Sky Park, a large terrace on the tower's ninth floor. True to the station's name, which means "riverside," the terrace had a viewing platform that looked out over the Hangang River to the Jamsil and Olympic Bridges, with their eponymous neighborhoods beyond. What had been merely flurries an hour ago had by then turned into a full-blown snowstorm, and traffic crossing the Hangang River had slowed to a crawl; it was going to be a slow trip for anyone departing the terminal. With the snow coming down heavy, all I could see past the river's near bank was a screen of white. The cars and buses, and even the bridges themselves, gradually faded out of view before vanishing completely about halfway across, and it was as if the world beyond the river didn't exist at all.

Key places: East Seoul Bus Terminal, Techno Mart

ON AND OFF THE AVENUE

The thin line between two worlds in Gangnam

Arriving at Nonhyeon around noon, I emerged from the station to find the morning's rains stopped and a bright midday sun glinting off puddles and still-wet street signs. What had looked like it would be a gloomy, damp day had been transformed into the perfect weather for Nonhyeon's signature sport: armoire hunting.

The stretch of road between Nonhyeon and Hak-dong Stations forms Nonhyeon Furniture Street, and for several blocks, both sides of the avenue were lined with almost nothing but furniture stores. They were mostly of the high-end variety, which is what you'd expect in Seoul's posh Gangnam district. Several shops carried domestically made products whose style reflected Asian influence, but most seemed to supply imported pieces or work that was heavily cued by European design, shorthand for refinement to many Koreans. It was a predilection reflected in a quick scan of store names: F. Angelico, Maison Française, Italiano, Leicht, Giotto.

Many of these places had classy, elegant furniture in classy, elegant buildings, but there was also the occasional Old World mistake: Museo's façade was designed to look like a classical Italian villa, but the shoddy execution made it appear as if it had been constructed with a mix of plaster of Paris and frosting. It didn't help either that the embellishment didn't extend to the building's sides, leaving its very utilitarian underlying brick structure clearly visible. Inside, the furniture reflected the tastes of someone whose primary interest in fairy tales was aspirational. The store's display window was dominated by a giant bed whose gold bedposts, velvet headboard, and maroon velvet bedspread were almost absurdly over the top. Gawking at it, a friend asked if I could ever have sex in something like that. No way. Not unless I was given the title of Baron von Gangnam or something first. It would be too ridiculous otherwise; I'd start laughing in the middle and wouldn't be able to stop.

While it may not connote good taste, a bed like that does (insistently, adamantly) connote that the person sleeping in it is *RICH!*, and a store like Museo connoted the same about the neighborhood, which is how one usually thinks of Gangnam. Sometimes, however, the distance between two worlds is only a few steps.

Down Hakdong-ro 2-gil, a very un-Gangnam area was on display at Yeongdong Market. A typical neighborhood market, there were storefronts and street displays set up selling bedding, rice cakes, large primary-colored plastic bowls for washing and rinsing, and dozens of silver, finger-sized eels slithering in a bucket of aerated water.

While not particularly unique in and of itself, what was striking about the market was how utterly removed it felt from Gangnam's bustle and hum, an unassuming rebuttal to notions of a uniform neighborhood. A block away was not just Furniture Street but also Gangnam-daero, heavy with international chain stores and the traffic of German cars. In Yeongdong Market, though, that all disappeared. The streets were narrow, and the sound of traffic was gone. The majority of the people around were old men and women, indifferent to the teak nightstands two blocks away, preoccupied only with the buckets of fresh crabs at their feet.

Key places: Nonhyeon Furniture Street, Yeongdong Market

WATERWORLD

*Palace intrigue and the wet charm of
Noryangjin Fisheries Wholesale Market*

Before going to Noryangjin for the first time several years ago, my assumption was that the neighborhood surrounding Seoul's largest fish market would be correspondingly wet, grimy, and smelly. Not so.

The scene along Noryangjin-ro was bright and clean and, to my surprise, the smell filling the air wasn't the dank, salty tang of fish but the scents pouring out of the long row of street food stalls lining the south side of the avenue, each one with a cartoon bear and sign at its top proclaiming "Happy Dongjak!" in reference to the surrounding district. While the standard trio of spicy rice cakes, dumplings, and blood sausage was present, the fare here was more varied than usual and tilted more toward quick lunches than snacks. I passed carts offering *bibimbap*, *bulgogi* hot dogs, hamburgers, *omurice* (fried rice wrapped in an omelet), and something that one cart called "bomb rice."

I'd never heard of that last one before, and, being a sucker for both spicy food and street eating, I ordered up. What I got was a bowl of rice with ground beef, sesame oil, processed cheese, fried egg, two different kinds of dried seaweed, some fish roe, two generous dollops of red pepper paste, and a sprinkling of sesame seeds. Total cost: KRW 2,000, or less than two dollars. And how was it? A delicious mess, which is to say: pure Korean comfort food.

Not wanting to confront the odor of thousands of fish so soon after eating, I instead made my way east down Noryangjin-ro to Sayuksin Park.

A year or so earlier, while visiting the Changsin neighborhood, I'd come across a place called Jeongeobwon, the site where Queen Jeongsun (1440–1521) had lived, mourning her husband, the boy-king Danjong. King Danjong had ascended to the throne at all of 12 years old, after his father had fallen ill and died just two years after taking power. Prepubescent kings tend to suffer complicated relations with their relatives, and Danjong was no exception. He was usurped, exiled, and then murdered in 1457 by his uncle, who then became King Sejo. Following Danjong's overthrow, an attempt was made by six ministers to restore him to the throne. Their plot was betrayed, however, and while one of the officials opted to commit suicide rather than face the inevitable consequences, the other five were tortured and executed. In a tactic mirrored by the North Korean regime centuries later, this punishment was extended to many of the conspirators' family members. After their deaths, the men subsequently became known as the Sayuksin, the Six Martyred Ministers.

This park was where the sordid little tale came full circle.

After their deaths, four of the ministers were buried here, on the southern banks of the Hangang River, well outside the city walls. In 1681, King Sukjong ordered a school to be built on the site as a memorial to the men's loyalty and valor. Today the tombs are recognized prosaically as Seoul Tangible Cultural Property No. 8. On the day I visited the site, red-and-blue lanterns hung in front of the traditional wooden shrine, and, inside, seven simple wood tablets rested on a long burgundy altar. A half dozen joss sticks smoldered in a brass urn, their sweet aroma drifting through the tranquil setting. Behind the shrine and through a door in a stone wall was the cemetery. Four tumuli sat on a grassy knoll surrounded by fir trees, while a few steps northwest sat three more, each with a small stone marker in front of it. Yes, your math is correct—six ministers, seven tumuli. The Sayuksin were originally established as being Park Paeng-nyeon, Seong Sam-mun, Yi Gae, Yu Eung-bu—who are actually buried beneath their tombs—and Ha Wi-ji, and Yu Seong-won—who are not. But later scholars raised doubts about the veracity of Yu Eung-bu's inclusion, positing that the sixth man was actually another minister named Kim Mun-gi. The question could never be answered definitively, so in 1977, as a mathematically smudgy compromise, a seventh tomb was constructed.

Leaving the park, I headed back toward the station, to where an elevated walkway led over some rail tracks. If you make that same walk now, what you'll notice first is a large, sleek glass-and-metal structure with a sign saying Noryangjin Fisheries Wholesale Market. This is the market's new home, built at a cost of over KRW 200 billion (USD 170 million) and opened in early 2016. At the time I first visited it wasn't there, and the market operated out of its old, airplane hangar–like warehouse. Even a few months after the new building opened, however, there remained the question of just how "there" it was. Citing less floor space and increased rents in the new structure, roughly 60 percent of Noryangjin's merchants were refusing to move in, continuing to work in the old space.

I reached that old space via the elevated walkway, which put me on the market's second floor. Before descending I paused to take in the spectacle from above, in order to get an idea of both the market's size and structure. From above, Noryangjin resembled nothing so much as the grid of an urban marine metropolis, divided into blocks by the wet concrete aisles, those blocks further subdivided into lots of individual stalls, and those lots divided again into apartments housing all manner of fish, sea squirts, clams, and cockles. Traffic consisted of small flatbed trucks piled high with huge bags of ice that periodically drove by, unloading the material that kept the entire system in equilibrium. (One wonders how many kilograms of ice the market goes through in a single day.) And just like a city, underneath all of this the market had its own aural signature, composed of the squeak of Styrofoam, the rip of packing tape, the faint bubbling of aerators, and the continual chatter of the men and women overseeing it all.

Down on the floor, the wet city came into full relief. It was surprising to witness just how neatly the amorphous forms of squid and octopi could be laid out by professionals, and these, along with the geometric tanks and tidy piles of clams and oysters, made Noryangjin more orderly than I'd expected a fish market had any right to be. Above each little stand hung several lamps and a sign or two with the stall's name, and below there were prawns the size of bananas, pulsing squid, and lazily waving tentacles. At some stalls, recycling water cascaded from one tank to the next like wedding champagne over tiered flutes, and the air in the market was so moist that, rather than feeling as if water had been added to every available container that could hold it, it felt as though the water had somehow been removed from the space I stood in, Moses-like.

The damp, the salt, the smell, the slipperiness—the inherent features of docks and seafood markets mean there's no way to beautify them, but that handicap is also precisely their charm. All too often, life in Seoul can feel excessively superficial—the copious plastic surgery ads, the requisite head shots on job applications—but walking amid the market stalls and their workers served as a powerful detoxicant, a reminder that those concerns aren't universal. Here, the dress code tended toward fishing vests, Wellingtons, and rubber gloves. Vanity and the transport of cephalopods may not be mutually exclusive, but they are certainly infrequent associates.

Everywhere around me the rubber-armored brigade was busy at work. An elderly woman knifed open clams. Vendors used flat, wooden mallets to pound and smooth out ice. A man at a band saw cut frozen fish into fist-size chunks. Middle-aged women operated small stands selling instant coffee and ramen to the workers. Crowbar-shaped picks got swung to lift, to drag, to open boxes, to move fish. Men driving trucks and mopeds zipped around, taking things from Point A to Point B, and sinewy porters pulling heavily loaded dollies did the same.

In a large open space at the west end of the market was the auction area. Guys wearing plain baseball hats with numbers on the front wandered around, the numbers their IDs for the auction where the day's catch was to be sold off. About 2:30 a.m., a large clatter began as hundreds of identical yellow bins started getting unstacked, tossed onto the floor, and filled with water. This was where the lots got placed—one flopping fish each if it was big;

three, four, five of them if they were smaller; mesh bags filled with dozens of eels. Elsewhere, large octopi were laid out alongside sleek, beautiful, meter-long tunas. In the earliest of early morning hours, all of these would be called out, bid on, and sold to someone who would become the next link in the chain from sea to plate.

It's possible to shorten that chain considerably, and even at 3 a.m. there were people arriving at the market to do just that, some of them clearly having made the transition directly from the club. Although the second-floor restaurants were closed, many fishmongers had plates stacked up and ready to go right next to the tanks, more than happy to slice up a purchase right then and there.

Many still are. While the new building is now up and running, the old one isn't dead, not yet. Its holdouts continue their standoff with the National Federation of Fisheries Cooperative, which manages the market, keeping the old place alive for the time being. In Korea, this type of standoff between labor and management is a common one, and will inevitably end with the vendors either begrudgingly moving into the new building—perhaps with lowered rents or increased compensation—or leaving and trying to restart their business somewhere else. The new building will likely work out fine, but it won't have the old one's grit or its indifference to appearance, and I for one will miss that.

Key places: Noryangjin-dong street food stalls, Sayuksin Park, Noryangjin Fisheries Wholesale Market

HERE TODAY, GONE TOMORROW

Never the same neighborhood twice

The moment someone sits down at a keyboard and tries to describe a place, it's already a little bit gone—no longer the place it was when it was seen. Unavoidable and just fine, really. It clears the way for new records, allows for comparisons (maybe even lessons or conclusions), and means that new words and new books and new describers are always needed. But when a place changes as fast as Seoul does, it can sometimes feel like a new version is needed before the old one is even finished. The best one can do is to settle for providing a snapshot of a particular moment, even if the expiration date has already passed and what used to be there is already gone. That's just the way it is with Seoul, some neighborhoods even more than others.

Sangsu, for one.

The area around Hongik University, Korea's top school for art, is known colloquially as Hongdae and is the wellspring for much of the country's independent and underground art, music, and culture. I lived in the neighborhood for a couple of years and continue to go back frequently, and every time I do something has changed. A new store's gone in, an old restaurant has moved out, an entire building has gone up or come down. And as corporations have rushed to capitalize on the area's cachet as the country's coolest neighborhood, many of its small, idiosyncratic, and quirky features have been pushed out to its edges, to neighborhoods like Sangsu, changing them drastically in the process.

During one visit, the area south of the station and Dongmak-gil gave an interesting but subtle picture of what was taking shape there. When I walked through the backstreets, at first glance things looked exactly as they did in dozens and dozens of other mostly residential areas of Seoul: quiet-ish one-and-a-half-lane streets surrounded by middle-class redbrick apartment buildings. But then I started to notice little things that betrayed the influence of the university just a few blocks away: hipster bike shops, vintage boutiques, small galleries, small cafés, small gallery-cafés. One of these had a folding sign on the alley outside that read almost like a haiku:

Don't honk
We are making
A beautiful
Alley

But in a cheeky and very Hongdae touch, the little lyric was accompanied by a picture of two stick figures—one on its knees, the other looming over its head, arm raised and baton cocked.

They really meant it.

If the changes taking place southwest of the station were subtle, those to the southeast were anything but. There, the neighborhood was undergoing a facelift. Walking around, the green, black, and pink striped blankets put up around construction sites in Korea were a common sight, and quite a few small businesses had closed up. Many of these, and many houses as well, had the word 철거 (demolition) slashed across their windows and sides in red spray paint. Nestled on plum real estate between Hongdae and the Hangang River, those buildings' days had likely been numbered for quite some time.

While the area south of the station drops hints of the university's influence, the area to the north is distinctly part of what is considered Hongdae. You'll know where you are by the abundance of wall murals and colorful street paintings that pop up most everywhere you go. There's what's known as "Mural Alley" running just south of the university's main gate, but sections of this were torn down, and the paintings there were never among the area's best anyway, those being scattered elsewhere throughout the neighborhood. To name just a small sampling of what I saw as I wandered, there were power line poles decorated in tiger stripes and Super Mario motifs, grinning cats with angel wings, dragons and ogres on acid trips, 30-eyed swamp things swinging by on jungle vines, and a mutant grandmother, permed and lipsticked, but also fanged, warted, and bloodied.

Cutting through the heart of Hongdae is a road that's just known as Parking Street, and it possesses what must be the world's greatest discrepancy between the coolness of a street and the coolness of its name. Alive at any time, on weekend nights it's a midway of the hippest kids in the city eating at food stalls, shopping at boutiques, heading to clubs, busking for spare change, and wearing clothes and hairstyles way better than yours. If you can pull yourself away from the spectacle, the area between Parking Street, the university, and the station is one of Seoul's most serendipitous, and an afternoon's exploration could very likely turn up your new favorite café, restaurant, shop, or all three. The best way to conduct oneself there—the only way, really, since there's a pretty high likelihood that what's there today won't be there six months from now—is to simply wander about, let your ears absorb the ambient music, abandon any notion of trying to *find* something, and just let the neighborhood come to you. Do this and you may luck your way into an aromatic tea shop filled with ceramic cups and satchels of full-leaf teas, a clothing store selling playful sailor dresses and French raw denim, or a gastronomic ice cream shop serving scoops in flavors like Lebanese rosewater or Chinese five-spice squash. You'll also find places like the artisanal boulangerie and patisserie Publique, where loaves of dark bread dusted in flour sit in the window, displayed next to certificates from French baking schools—evidence that their rolls and baguettes are the real deal, a relative rarity in a country where "bread" usually means something white and sweet.

One place for which it's wise to abandon merely wandering in favor of actively seeking is Hakatabunko, home to the best Japanese ramen in Seoul. The fact that it's Zagat rated and almost always has a line out the door bodes well for it still being there by the time you read this, too.

Along with a couple of other dishes, Hakatabunko serves two types of ramen: one in a pork broth that's rich and full, the other a milder and lighter mix of pork and chicken. Both are incredibly savory, the noodles cooked to the perfect firmness. There are about four tables inside, but if you can, you'll want to grab a seat at the counter, where dozens of small toy figurines—Keroro,

Sailor Moon, the Catbus from *My Neighbor Totoro*—sit on a ledge above it. There you can watch the action taking place in the open kitchen in front of you. With a rolled bandanna tied around his head and sleeves pushed up sinewy arms, the chef boils noodles, pours broth, and garnishes dishes in a practiced and seemingly reflexive series of motions, all the while barking out welcomes and dish announcements in a loud Japanese rasp.

And that's the neighborhood. Or at least it was. In a place as quicksilver as Sangsu, there's every possibility that things are now totally different. But that's what makes Seoul Seoul, and what makes living or visiting here so endlessly interesting. You try to know the city, but she'll never really let you. The best you can hope to do is to keep coming back, keep reacquainting yourself, and take solace in the knowledge that there are, in fact, some things about her that don't change: the slow march of the Han, the sly glee of kids with paint, the simple perfection of steam pouring off a hot bowl of noodles.

Key places: Publique, Hakatabunko

SNAPSHOTS

What you're shown and what you see are
only the beginning of the story

Sometime in the late afternoon, the sun hits at the right angle and catches the new, nearly identical office towers west of the Nambusunhwan-ro highway, making them gleam as if the tech companies housed inside were lighting the way to the future, which, I suppose, is kind of the whole idea.

About 50 years ago, at the start of Korea's great developmental push, the Guro Industrial Complex was built in the area around the neighborhoods of Guro and Garibong. As Korea's economic growth continued, though, many of the factories decamped, mostly overseas. Electronics assembly, textiles, and factories were out, IT companies were in. There are now more than 8,000 in the area, making it the country's largest concentration of tech labor, and they employ over 100,000 workers creating everything from digital content to semiconductors.

It's a remarkable economic transformation, and Seoul loves to shine a spotlight on this side of itself—its superfast Internet connections, its digital sorcery, its life lived on a touch screen. This is fair enough, as it's all true, but it's not a complete portrait of the city or even this particular neighborhood. The office towers and the area immediately around them hold little of interest for the casual visitor, and to focus on them alone leaves out Namguro's most interesting, most entertaining aspects, like showing guests the newly remodeled house but not the family photo album. To see those snapshots, to turn those pages, one must turn corners.

Leaving the shining towers behind, I crossed to the highway's other side, where a half dozen old women sat in a cluster on the sidewalk alongside bundles of onions and other vegetables, peeling garlic. Around them, the grubby neighborhood was filled with rough convenience stores, pet shops, fried chicken joints, and cheapo salons. Just steps from the station was a row of seven hostess bars, followed immediately by a church. Sin, repent, repeat.

Up and down the street, shop signs were scrawled with Chinese characters, a visual counterpart to the dipping and rising tones coming from the neighborhood's Chinese and *joseonjok*, or Korean-Chinese, population. It was one of several such communities on Seoul's southwest side, a loose constellation of not-quite Chinatowns that many Seoulites view with a mixture of suspicion and disregard. There were no temples to Tian Hou or kitschy Mao souvenirs, but there were Chinese karaoke rooms, Chinese realtors, and Chinese restaurants offering foods that either occupied the fringes of Korean cuisine or were missing from it entirely: dog meat, grilled lamb, catfish, Szechuan hot pot. Occasionally the sharp-sweet odor of star anise cut through the air.

Down a side street, a shopping cart and suitcase leaned up against each other outside an apartment building. Next to them a rusty bike was chained to a second suitcase, another rusty bike was locked to a rustier clothes rack, and a third rusty bike was locked to a milk crate and toppled parking sign. I walked further, and just past that oxidized triptych came across a play set in the shape of a giant chicken, roosting in the middle of a day care center playground.

These images were parts of Namguro that Seoul would never call attention to, but they were nevertheless pieces of it, embedded in the pages of the city's scrapbook and causing one to wonder about the stories behind them: How did those things come to be there? How did those people live? For me, the scrapbook's most yellowed, most dog-eared pages—the ones that seemed most pregnant with stories—were the ones that opened to scenes from Guro Market. The first image was a tarp-covered alley leading in, lined with clothing shops offering *hanbok*, or traditional Korean clothing, and the sorts of pieces that appeal to the over-50 set here: obnoxious floral patterns, sequins, elastic waistbands, colors that seem to be used together out of mere spite, as if the designer, vowing revenge on the haute couture world that rejected her, chose the most offensive combinations possible.

That alley ended at a section of the market covered by an arched corrugated metal roof. There were no ceiling lights, only bare bulbs and fluorescent tubes hanging over individual stalls, so even though it was the middle of the afternoon and the sun was shining, the market remained dark.

Continuing on brought me to the next image: a huddle of small restaurants and food stalls. Each had a linoleum countertop with wooden benches on one, two, or three sides, usually with a blanket held in place by packing tape for cushioning. Glass display cases on the countertops showed what was on offer, TVs were tuned to baseball games or variety shows, and in the center of each stall one or two women alternately cooked on small gas burners and gabbed with the clientele. Food was unfussy: chicken feet, clams, squid. There was a pile of crabs, one still moving, just a bit. There were almost no amenities, seemingly no concern for any health regulations, no shine or sheen, but the food satisfied and nobody asked for more than that.

Past the food stalls and back in the sunlight were vegetables, fish, and cylinders of dry noodles wrapped in butcher paper with the names of their type scrawled in magic marker on the side. There were grandparents, lone mothers, and whole families together, and stalls and stalls beyond them. What had looked small from that first alley kept revealing new spaces, new scenes, expanding beyond its expected boundaries and hinting at yet more stories.

Key place: Guro Market

LIFE BELOW THE MOUNTAINS

A slower pace on the edge of town

A half dozen fish were drying out in front of a restaurant. They'd been tied up with string laced through their mouths and gills and hung from a pipe balanced between two plastic chairs, waiting patiently for the sun to do its slow work. It might be the mellowing influence of the mountains, or maybe it's just being on the edge of the city, but Danggogae is like that. It's sleepy. It's quiet there. A few people may be out snacking at fast food stalls or doing their shopping for the week, but no one is in much of a rush to get anywhere. It's a Sunday kind of neighborhood, even on Mondays.

As is the case with so many of the communities on Seoul's outer edges, Danggogae sits in the shadow of nearby mountains—Mt. Buramsan to the southeast and Mt. Suraksan to the north. On the street, brightly clad hikers were either on their way to or from the peaks, and just outside the station the neighborhood's charms were already evident. The air in Danggogae was less polluted than in other parts of Seoul, and lovely views of Mt. Buramsan's forested peak rose up beyond the buildings, its bald northwestern face sticking out like the bare strip cut by a razor through a thick beard.

Tucked between the peak and the station was a jumble of low-income homes, and I would have likely missed the tiny neighborhood altogether had I not noticed the patchwork of rooftops through the windows of the elevated train platform. Many of the houses had tarps on their roofs that were held down by bricks or tiles or, in some instances, by pumpkins being grown up there. After finding my way into the neighborhood, I noticed more vegetables drying on blankets spread out in front of doors. One resident had repurposed a clothes rack by slinging a reed mat across its arms and spreading out zucchini slices. Mixed in among the houses were a number of *mudangjib*, the homes of female shamans, with red-and-white flags hung outside announcing their presence like semaphores.

Walking around the area, just south of the tracks, I could hear the arriving and departing trains and the bells and announcements drifting over from the station. For me, it was a cheerful sound in the late afternoon light, but I doubted that the neighborhood's residents, exposed to it from dawn until midnight, felt the same. In addition to the noise, another problem that they were clearly trying to cope with was the cold. Homes in these types of neighborhoods rarely have modern heating systems, their warmth instead provided by old-fashioned charcoal briquettes. For that there was the neighborhood briquette hut, with hundreds of cylinders stacked up, ready for winter. Hung on the front of the hut was a small whiteboard on which someone had written a phone number for orders.

In contrast to the modest southern section, a short walk under the tracks to the west brought me to one of the fancier neighborhood parks I'd ever come across. There was an artificial waterfall opposite the main entrance, and the central cascade, flanked by two smaller ones, tumbled into a small pool, kicking up a very fine mist. Above the waterfall was a small wooden pavilion, which a group of boys had commandeered and turned into a fort, and behind that were some stone steps marking the beginning of a path toward the foot of Mt. Suraksan. In the opposite corner of the park was a climbing wall, the yellow tower sticking up above many of the surrounding trees. About 20 climbers were hanging around, taking turns scaling its pebbled face, acting as spotters, and relaxing on mats and lawn chairs around the edge of the padded base.

More leisurely recreation was being pursued back on a traffic median running alongside the station, where several congregations of old men were sitting on park benches or just standing around. A couple of these groups, numbering about a dozen each, were either participating in or watching competitive games of *yunnori*, a traditional game where two-sided sticks are tossed like dice. Others were taking in games of go or *janggi*, Korean chess, while one group had done away with the pretense altogether and was just sitting around drinking. And why not? In Danggogae, there was nowhere they needed to be, nothing they needed to do.

Key place: Danggogae Park

INDEPENDENCE MOVEMENT

*A 400-year struggle for freedom,
and the legacy of impermanence it left behind*

On a May evening in the spring of 1592, vessels carrying 7,000 Japanese soldiers landed at the port city of Busan, initiating what would come to be known as the Imjin War: six years of invasions intended to conquer Joseon Korea and, eventually, Ming China. After laying siege to Busan, the Japanese forces swept north toward present-day Ulsan and soon arrived at Tongdosa Temple, Korea's largest, nestled in the foothills of Mt. Sinbulsan. In the course of laying waste to both buildings and inhabitants, they also saw fit to relieve the temple of its most prized possession: a tooth that had reputedly belonged to the Buddha himself. Predictably, this did not sit well with the country's monks, among them Great Master Samyeong, the head priest at Geonbongsa Temple on Mt. Geonbongsan, close to what's now the border with North Korea.

A figure straight out of central casting, draped in robes and a long flowing beard, he responded by assembling a militia of fighting monks, a collection of holy warriors that ultimately helped expel the invaders from the peninsula. Following the war's conclusion, in 1604, Samyeong traveled to Japan as an envoy of the Korean government and met with Tokugawa Ieyasu, the ruling Japanese shogun. It's impossible to know exactly what Samyeong said in that meeting, but it ended with Tokugawa returning both the tooth and 3,500 Korean prisoners, which, it must be said, is not a bad day's work. A statue of Samyeong now stands near the entrance to Dongguk University, Korea's most prestigious Buddhist school, the monk's right hand holding a staff, his left placed over his heart.

Past the monk, the Dongguk campus itself is largely unremarkable; many of its buildings are bland in a 1960s kind of way common to Korean universities, but it is home to one structure of great significance. Built between 1617 and 1620, Sungjeongjeon Hall was the main hall of Gyeonghuigung Palace, one of five royal residences in downtown Seoul. It was in Sungjeongjeon that three kings were crowned and where they and others held official ceremonies and entertained foreign emissaries. Following the Japanese annexation of Korea in 1910, Gyeonghuigung was largely destroyed and a middle school was built in its place. The hall was moved to Jogyesa Temple and then, in 1976, moved again to its present location. The brightly painted structure is now called Jeonggagwon and used as Dongguk University's sermon hall.

Before my first visit to the Jangchung area, as this part of town is known, my knowledge of it was limited to the odd couple institutions with which the area is most closely associated: the Buddhist university and pork trotter restaurants, the latter of which cluster on the first block or two north of the station. Most of them have some combination of the words "fat," "original," and "grandma" in their names, and with so little to separate them, they all employ barkers to work the sidewalks, trying to cajole pedestrians into their respective establishments.

When I got to the neighborhood, however, I was surprised by a third quality: how insistently it kept alive the history of past independence activists. Samyeong was merely the first in a long line of freedom fighters that have been memorialized in this part of the city.

Below the university was Jangchungdan Park, which was filled with shrines and statues. Occupying an open space in the center was the Jangchungdan Monument, a stone tablet erected by Emperor Gojong in 1900 to soothe the spirits of those victimized during the Eulmi Sabyeon, the tumultuous period in 1895 during which Empress Myeongseong was assassinated and many soldiers were killed fighting the Japanese in a futile effort to keep Korea's sovereignty from slipping away. Of course, once that fight was lost and annexation was complete, the stone was removed. It was only after World War II that it was finally replaced, returned to what is now the site of the Shilla Hotel (just across Jangchungdan-gil) before eventually being brought back to its original location in 1969, not far from where the royal guard station Namsoyeong once stood.

On the park's west side sat a trio of monuments, one being a statue of politician "Ilseong" Yi Jun. Born in 1859, Yi was a member of the Independence Association, and in 1907 received an order from Emperor Gojong to participate in the International Peace Conference being held in The Hague. Unable to enter due to Japanese obstruction, Yi sought recourse by going to the press, appealing to world leaders to recognize the Eulsa Treaty, which had formalized annexation, as void and to denounce the Japanese invasion. Though the press was sympathetic, world powers ignored Yi's case. Yi died shortly after this rejection, and the cause of death remains clouded by uncertainty. Theories range from assassination by Japanese spies to suicide by disembowelment to what Koreans call *bunsa*, death by disappointment. The fact that for decades Yi's body remained in the Netherlands only added to the mystery. It wasn't until 1963 that his remains were returned to Korea.

Several meters north was the "Monument of Korean Confucian Scholars' Independence Movement by Long Letter to Paris," which was, above all, a mouthful. The letter in question was sent to the Paris Peace Conference around the time of the March 1, 1919 independence movement, asking for the conference's support. Signed by 137 Confucian scholars, it was delivered by Kim Gyusik, a delegate of the provisional government in Shanghai.

The independence struggle was not the only history represented in the park, though. On its eastern edge, a man-made stream ran under wooden footbridges and trees leaning out over the water, over a series of little cascades, around a small circular island, and past thick bunches of tawny reeds with wispy gray tops. It also passed below the 27.5-meter granite Supyo Bridge, constructed during the first half of the 15th century, and originally spanning the Cheonggyecheon Stream. When the Cheonggyecheon underwent its postwar redevelopment in 1959, the bridge was moved, and then moved again to its present location in 1965.

From the park, I followed Jangchungdan-gil south as it ran between the stream and the silver roof of Jangchung Gymnasium, Korea's first domed gymnasium and now host to volleyball, basketball, handball, and *ssireum*, a traditional Korean form of wrestling. Skirting the eastern side of Mt. Namsan, the road brought me to a statue of Yu Gwan-sun, rushing forward, torch held aloft. A student activist and independence agitator, Yu is one of Korea's most famous martyrs. Following March 1, 1919 protests she helped organize, she was arrested, thrown in Seodaemun Prison, tortured, and killed at the age of 17. A few dozen meters further on was the Commemorative Monument Tower of March 1 Korean Independence Declaration. Standing 19.19 meters tall (to honor 1919, the year the statement was issued), the large stone tower came to a sharp point at the top, resembling a weaponized fountain pen. There's inevitably a certain amount of aggression inherent in any declaration of independence, but I felt like that aggression came across too forcefully in the monument, leaving no space for the aspiration or optimism that are also innate to any such proclamation.

My visit to the Jangchung area had turned into a heavier afternoon than I'd expected, and I needed to clear my head a bit. Not far from the gymnasium was a restored section of the old city wall, and I followed the signs to the trail alongside it, tracing the path as it curved upward until I found myself on a small ridge, alone and surrounded by quiet for the first time all day. It was starting to get dark, and the lights in the apartment towers to the east were switching on, making the structures look like electric checkerboards. Just to the north, barkers tried to hustle passersby into restaurants, and, beyond them, the neon lights of Dongdaemun's all-night shopping towers were already ablaze.

Over 400 years had passed since the Buddha's tooth was stolen and then recovered, and that was only the first in a long procession of things that had been removed, returned, or relocated: Sungjeongjeon Hall, the Jangchungdan Monument, Supyogyo Bridge, Yi Jun's body. Even something as permanent-seeming as the wall behind me had been partially razed and redone and rebuilt, and all these changes made me wonder how much that legacy of impermanence had seeped into the Korean psyche. If walls and teeth and bodies were so inconstant, then didn't everything, from the trivial—money, beauty, customers—to the priceless—sovereignty, democracy, independence—have to be pursued with determined urgency, chased after as if it could disappear at any moment?

Key places: Dongguk University, Sungjeongjeon Hall, pork trotter restaurants, Jangchungdan Park, Supyogyo Bridge, Jangchungdan Monument, Jangchung Gymnasium, Statue of Yu Gwan-sun, Commemorative Monument Tower of March 1 Korean Independence Declaration, Seoul City Wall Trail

TRACK

Identity changes, for a station and an athlete,
decades in the making

More than other types of transportation, trains possess a certain romance. When the first commercial airlines began crossing the Atlantic, their exclusivity and the ease with which they linked exotically named cities momentarily gave flight an unmatched glamor; few, however, still find any remnants of this in contemporary air travel, with its steadily decreasing comforts and increasing security indignities. And whereas flights—with their unnatural relation to time and lack of any reference linking the points of departure and arrival—can feel like a very long intermission between acts, travel by train proceeds recognizably through time and space, giving it a natural sense of narrative. In movies, planes lend themselves to action or comedy; trains to drama and mystery. As for boat travel, in developed countries it's a relative rarity, and cruises aren't so much transportation as the vacation itself: floating hotels-cum-theme parks for retirees. Trains alone still evoke a sense that wonderful things might happen not only at your destination but on your way there. Connecting one's ordinary life to a new place, a new setting, they suggest a story unfolding, something that's reflected in the titles of the great routes: the Orient Express, the Trans-Siberian, the Blue Train, the Ghan. It's no coincidence that the Hogwarts Express was a steam engine: magical people take the train.

Sadly, Korean rail travel's possibilities are shackled by political realities. But should reunification ever occur, the country could become the terminus for what would undoubtedly be one of the world's longest and most incredible journeys: Lisbon to Seoul overland.

While the country's railroad suffers in its geographical limitations, its capital is at least home to a wonderful station. Or, rather, stations.

The new Seoul Station is a modern exemplar: bright and airy, bustling but uncongested. It's filled with restaurants, shops, and corporate displays, but the tall, high windows create a feeling of space, and people move through the station efficiently.

I'd come to the station not to travel anywhere, but merely to observe people who were, and, for a while at least, to imagine myself among them. After drifting through the concourse, I decided to head out to the mezzanine above the tracks, where I could watch the flow of trains pulling in and out and passengers boarding and disembarking. I was almost there when a yellow line on the ground caused me to stop short. On it was a string of Korean text with an English translation that read, "We Trust You: (Only paid customers can cross this line)." It took me a moment to realize that this was the security check. All of it. There were no guards, no metal detectors, no baggage inspection. It was remarkable, and even though I had no intention of sneaking onto a train, the yellow line seemed so good-natured, so trusting, so esteeming of my character that it actually made me pause and consider whether or not I should cross it. When I did, I needed to convince myself that what I was doing was OK, that I was acting in the name of reportage and not actually doing anything wrong.

Outside, below the woven gray canopy of beams, trains lined up on the tracks—evenly spaced silver tubes, like the pipes of an organ. I found a spot near the mezzanine's edge to watch as a stream of hundreds of dark coats poured out of a newly arrived train and up the escalators. It was New Year's Eve, and many of the country's conscripted soldiers were out on leave, heading home to see their families. A group of about 20 army men went by, all dressed in identical camouflage fatigues, green canvas duffels strapped to their backs. More stylish were the marines in natty gray topcoats with polished gold buttons.

Located directly beside the new terminal, the old Seoul Station is a beauty of a thing. Designed by the Japanese architect Tsukamoto Yasushi and completed in 1925, it looks the way a train station is supposed to look. Thick stone slabs ring the bottom below reddish-pink bricks, all underneath an arched central window and Byzantine dome.

While trains may no longer run from the old station, it has fortunately been brought back to life with an extensive refurbishment and reimagining. Reopened in 2011 and somewhat clumsily rechristened Culture Station Seoul 284, its new life is as an exhibition space. And as interesting as the artwork was, the station itself was equally fascinating, if not more so. The new Seoul Station may be a paragon of modernity, but the original captures the imagination in a way unique to old rail stations. Thick granite

columns lined the foyer, and light streamed through a stained
-glass skylight in the ceiling. There were fireplaces, candelabras,
and wood paneling on the walls. It wasn't hard to envision a curl
of cigarette smoke drifting out from a shadowy corner, followed
by a trench-coated Graham Greene or Somerset Maugham.
Strolling the carpeted floor of what used to be The Grill—for a
long time Seoul's best Western restaurant—the ghosts of foreign
powers plotting Korea's fate in the prewar years seemed to hover
just out of view. There was at least one spot where the old station
offered an even deeper look into its past: in the old barber shop
and restroom on the second floor, refurbishment had been
deliberately left half-completed, providing a view of the building's
original construction materials and techniques.

The old and new stations are connected by Seoul Square,
which many Seoulites know primarily as a gathering spot for
the city's homeless. The Korean capital's homeless rate, when
viewed in comparison with American cities, is remarkably low:
approximately 3,300 as of 2012, including those living in shel-
ters, compared with 64,000 in New York City. Coming from the
United States, where urban poverty is both far more prevalent
and visible, the infrequency with which one encounters the
homeless in Seoul is surprising. The plaza here, however, is one
of the few places in this city of 10 million where the problem
is readily apparent, where those with no place to go can always
be found, wandering the square or sitting on cardboard eating
instant noodles. More were on the road leading south from the
plaza—one man squatting over a pile of discarded wires, peeling
the plastic coating off by hand to get at the valuable copper
inside, about 50 others queued up on the sidewalk, waiting their
turn to get into a soup kitchen operated out of a small storefront.
Workers in bright yellow jackets watched over the crowd, and

when someone had finished his or her meal and exited they guided the next person in.

I crossed back through Seoul Station to the west, a quiet, largely residential neighborhood. It was there, past warehouses for the National Theater Company of Korea and a hilly area of lower-class homes, that I found Sohn Kee-chung Athletic Park.

Born in 1912 in Sinuiju, in what's now North Korea, Sohn was arguably Korea's greatest Olympian. A gifted distance runner, he won the marathon at the 1936 Berlin Games, setting an Olympic record in the process. It should have been Korea's first Olympic medal, its first Olympic record, but it was neither. Its sights on mainland Asia, Japan had forcibly annexed the peninsula in 1910 and, having erased Korean sovereignty, began a campaign to do the same to Korean culture, Korean pride, and the Korean language. From that point on, the sweat, muscles, and speed of the colony's athletes were in service of the emperor. Not even their names were spared. In Berlin, Sohn Kee-chung was Son Kitei, and his medal and record were Japan's. On the medal stand, as the imperial anthem rang through the stadium, Sohn hung his head and raised the pin oak sapling he'd received as victor to his chest, covering the Japanese sun on the front of his uniform.

Amid the various athletic facilities in the park are two sculptures of Sohn. One is a large rendering solely of the elderly Sohn's head, looking out from the park's highest point over the rooftops of central Seoul. In front of the sculpture is the pin oak, planted here when the site was still Yangjeong High School, Sohn's alma mater. The second statue is partway down the slope, depicting the marathoner as he was on that day in 1936. Eighty years after the race, the International Olympic Committee still credits the gold medal to Japan, still recognizes its winner as Son Kitei. In the historical record, the only respite from this theft of identity might be found in the anonymity of the number on Sohn's racing bib, which is how he is identified on the statue: runner No. 382. He is midstride, his head cocked at a peculiar angle as he strains to outrun the other athletes and, just as surely, the shame and burden he was made to carry.

Key places: Seoul Station, Culture Station Seoul 284, Seoul Square, Sohn Kee-chung Athletic Park

URBAN PASTORAL

An autumn stroll

After summer ends and the burning Morse code of the neighborhood's cicadas begins to dissipate, Jamwon settles into an early fall that's crisp and clear and carries echoes of a country village. Instead of the major intersection one usually sees when emerging from a station's exit, here there were beds of shrubs and wildflowers, and daisies and berries grew parallel to a quiet, two-lane street bisected by a grassy median. The street was lined with gingko trees, and while those of nearby Garosu-gil are more celebrated, I found that an autumn stroll under Jamwon's marigold-flaked branches was a more tranquil walk, offering an intimate glimpse of a side of south bank life that usually gets overlooked. Near a blue-and-green statue of a smiling silkworm, a man sold oranges out of the back of a truck. Across the street, two grandmothers at a small produce stand sorted cabbages and zucchinis that had perhaps come straight from the small garden in the shade of a large willow tree just a dozen or so meters behind them. An old man had commandeered one of the sidewalk's wooden benches to set up an impromptu shoeshine and shoe repair business.

I could have spent the better part of the day just sitting at the bench's other end, and if I'd had more sense perhaps I would have, but I wanted to see what else the neighborhood had to offer, and so I set off toward the river.

After drifting through a few shady blocks between apartment complexes I was on Jamwon-ro, a large boulevard just south of the Hangang River. Given the calm of the area I'd just left, I wanted to find a quieter route, so I turned onto a short side street to the north. At the end of the laneway was a dirt path that ran parallel to Jamwon-ro, and I followed it east, through dappled shade thrown down by rows of perfectly spaced young pine trees. To my left, a towering concrete wall provided a barrier to the riverside Olympic Expressway, and though I could hear the rush of traffic moving just meters away, that bustle seemed irrelevant to the stillness of the wooded trail I found myself on.

A short ways down the path I came to an entrance to Hangang Park. After passing through a tunnel beneath the expressway I came out alongside the river, where the breeze kicked up and carried with it the soft *thwup* of rackets striking tennis balls. I passed people exercising and an old man rolling down the bike path on a tricycle. The Jamwon swimming pools, crowded with families and water wings in the summertime, had been drained in anticipation of the cold, but another riverside attraction (if you can call it that) was open. Underneath a model of a giant, arching silkworm was the Silkworm Experience Learning Center. In an area renowned for its silk production during the Joseon Dynasty, the center was a place where students and the occasional curious visitor could learn all about the insect's life and labors. That—labor—seemed like a terrible idea on a day like this. I decided to leave it to the worms and went back outside.

Key places: Jamwon Hangang Park, Silkworm Experience Learning Center

HOME IMPROVEMENT

*Home furnishings elevated to the level of art,
or science fiction*

The first time I came upon Nonhyeon Furniture Street I was surprised to find that Seoul had an entire street devoted to furniture. By the time I made it back, however, I'd been to three others, and the only thing that struck me as unique about Nonhyeon was that you could drop a lot more money there. But a turn down a random side street showed that Gangnam prices weren't the only thing setting Nonhyeon apart.

Less than a block off the main street was a boxy, modern, three-story building—part showroom, partworkshop. Hearing the buzz of power saws, not a common sound in Gangnam, I looked in at the first-floor shop, open to the street and full of very serious-looking equipment. An ornate, three-meter structure of steel tubes sat welded together on a giant table, like a clutch of drinking straws that had been dipped in silver paint.

On this particular day, I happened to be with a friend who'd studied furniture design in college, and she informed me that what we were looking at was the Choi Family Hardware Shop, a renowned hardware and design business. Now, hearing that a hardware shop is famous is a bit like hearing that someone is a celebrated model plane pilot—impressive to someone in the given field, but to anyone else the most typical response is probably the one I offered: raised eyebrows and a skeptical "Oh?"

It was only later that I came to understand that the Choi family shop is much more than your average nuts-and-bolts, six-jelly-donut-a-day staff kind of place. This isn't where you go to pick up flange nuts or a box-end wrench. The Chois' store is where you go if you're loaded and want to fit out your business with customized, one-of-a-kind tables, railings, or installations. It's furniture as art, a modern iteration of a legacy with deep roots on the peninsula. Along with the shop, the family also owns and runs the Lock Museum in the Daehangno neighborhood (where the Chois have also since relocated their business). On display are centuries-old boxes for cigarettes or *manggeon*, a men's hair accessory, carefully made in the shape of lotuses or fish, the latter a popular motif, as fish never close their eyes. The obvious skill and care that went into creating the old locks bestowed a sense of significance and value on whatever they might have protected, in marked contrast to today's digital barriers—our PIN codes and swipecards—which feel sterile, appropriate only for protecting commodities, data, or secrets.

The simple physicality of metalwork, the clear line that can be traced from a craftsman's hands to a box's latch, the emotional weight of the things we deem worth locking up—these are things that humans have understood for centuries, almost by instinct, and they're things that the work of artisans like the Chois allows us to reconnect with. For as masterly as their more elaborate pieces were—the giant steel straws, the hotel interiors—like the locks at the museum, it was their simple things that most impressed me, things like door handles more beautiful than I had thought a door handle could be, that on their own seemed able to transform the opening of a door from a simple mechanical act into the beginning of a story.

If hardware became something more than hardware in the hands of the Chois, bath fixtures became, well, *something* at Royal & Co. It was easy to spot the large gray and glass façade on Nonhyeon-ro, but far more indelible was what I saw inside: toilets, urinals, and showerheads lined up on a display floor like cars at an auto show. And, yes, it was as weird as it sounds. But even weirder was the fact that, after a few minutes, I had adjusted and started to admire the various ceramic structures, comparing their features and finding myself impressed by just what a toilet could do. And let's be honest—some of those showers were flat-out sexy.

In such a setting, mere passive admiration was hardly enough. I strolled past the polished stones in the reflecting pool to what is elsewhere known as a "restroom," but that here was so much more, as the sign reading "Experience Zone" clearly stated. I paused to admire the urinal artwork and then stepped into the bathroom. Inside, I was dealt an ego-bruising glimpse of how the Korean elite live, as the slightest touch triggered a motor to automatically raise the toilet seat, reminding me of the physical labor I was reduced to at home. I was humbled even further when I returned to the showroom, and another toilet's sensor, detecting my presence, initiated seat-raising without my even needing to lift a finger.

Should all that non-exertion work up the one percent's appetite, they wouldn't even need to page their chauffeurs, but could instead simply retire to the Italian restaurant on Royal & Co.'s second floor. I hear the food's good, but it's the ambiance that's truly special.

Key places: Nonhyeon Furniture Street, Royal & Co.

REMAINDERS

*Exploring the gritty remnants clinging on amid
Gongdeok's gentrification*

If someone were to blindfold you and then drop you off at the
intersection above Gongdeok Station, you could be forgiven for
thinking you were in the posh environs of Gangnam and not the
more humble Mapo-gu district. Mapo-ro is lined with sparkling
new buildings housing banks, restaurants, and cafés, and it's more
of the same along Baekbeom-ro—tall, modern structures with
the sorts of blandly humanistic sculptures that get commissioned
by corporate groups out front. There's a big blue man who looks
to be made out of lollipops holding a glowing white orb, and
metal stick figures running up a silver arc. The neighborhood
is starkly different from the much more modest areas nearby,
making it clear that Gongdeok has seen a lot of change, and seen
it fast. And with the recent additions of the Gyeongui-Jungang

and AREX lines and the station's subsequent transformation into one of the city's major transfer points, it's likely to see a lot more. But even the most modern and sterile neighborhoods in Seoul are not without their traces of grime or stubborn remainders from a rougher and not all that remote past.

For a better look at what the area was probably like a few years ago, I headed to Gongdeok Market, which was as old-school as could be. Its main alley was squeezed between a pair of old three-story brick buildings with tufts of grass and weeds growing out of cracks in their sides and roofs. Along the outside alley were piles of shoes and vegetable sellers and butchers whose cuts of meat were illuminated by lurid pink lights. Inside, dimly lit stalls occupied the first floor of a cramped, low-roofed building. Many were closed on the Sunday I visited, but some potent-smelling lunch booths were open and manned by wizened old women, though, to judge by the wail pouring from a second-story window, at least one of them had sneaked away to a *noraebang*, or Korean karaoke room.

I'd heard of the Gongdeok neighborhood being well known for a couple of foods, so one of my main goals for the visit was to sample them. Fortunately for serial eaters, the places to try both of these were right next to each other, occupying the market's outer edge.

As soon as I arrived I noticed several signs advertising *jokbal*, or pork trotters. The most prominent of these, and the one where a friend and I ate, was Gungjung Jokbal. It didn't appear all that big from the street, but once we were inside it revealed itself to be spread over about a half dozen rooms, as if the restaurant had undergone mitosis. Every single one of the rooms was boisterous and packed when we visited, as any good pork trotter place should be. *Jokbal* is one of the world's least pretentious eating experiences, and every time I have it I feel as if I really should have just finished working at the docks and should now be telling loud, off-color jokes. My longshoreman fantasy was graciously aided by the fact that a minute after we were seated two guys pulled up chairs at the table next to us, one of whom had the most spectacular mullet I'd ever seen in Korea. Less than 10 minutes later they had already started on their second bottle of soju.

Gungjung Jokbal's popularity probably owes quite a bit to its generosity. Along with a liberal portion of *jokbal*, the restaurant provided both a plate of *sundae* (blood sausage) and *sundae* soup free of charge. This might sound good in the abstract, but in practice, splitting all that nasty pork between two people can feel like eating your way toward your own death, and not slowly.

Less heart-attack-inducing (but only slightly) was what's referred to as Twigim Alley, just next to the *jokbal* places. This, however, was a total misnomer. Twigim Alley wasn't an actual alley of restaurants specializing in one food, like some other food streets in Seoul—Sindang's Tteokbokki Town or the mung bean pancake stalls in Gwangjang Market, to name a couple. It was just two big restaurants next to each other, each serving *twigim*, Korean tempura. The two restaurants, Cheonghakdong and Mapo Grandma Bindaetteok, sat on either side of a market alley and were each fronted by a long table piled with dozens of varieties of *twigim*. There was the standard assortment you see at any street cart—vegetable, potato, squid—but also less common offerings like hot pepper and perilla leaf—just about anything you could batter and deep-fry. The selection did not, however, extend to deep-fried Oreos or sticks of butter, leaving me reassured that America was still the undisputed deep-frying champion.

Pushing through the *jokbal* haze, my friend and I went to Cheonghakdong, where we loaded up a tray Dunkin' Donuts–

style and handed it over to the woman working the counter. Then we went upstairs to wait while our *twigim* was fried up. When the food came, along with a grease-splattered receipt, it was served with a cold radish kimchi soup, two other kinds of kimchi for cutting the grease, and soy sauce with onion slices for dipping the *twigim* in. We ordered a bottle of *makgeolli*, a milky rice wine that's the traditional drink of farmers and the perfect companion to *twigim*, and slumped onto the heated floor, beneath the rough-hewn wooden roof beams overhead. Regardless of what other changes came to Gongdeok, simple pleasures like this were certain to remain.

Key places: Gongdeok Market, Gungjung Jokbal, Cheonghakdong, Mapo Grandma Bindaetteok

HIDING IN PLAIN SIGHT

The many niches of downtown Seoul's overlooked corner

Despite sitting near the heart of downtown, the Euljiro 4-ga area had always remained off the radar for me. Surrounded by famous areas like Jongno, Myeong-dong, and Dongdaemun, it suffered from a Bermuda Triangle syndrome of sorts, disappearing amid the attractions of its better-known neighbors. Wanting to discover just what the neighborhood was all about, I hopped off the train one midwinter afternoon and decided to get lost for a few hours.

My timing could have been better. I'd moved into an unfurnished apartment a few months ago and had been acquiring furniture piecemeal, but had I visited earlier, or moved later, I could have taken care of everything all at once. Euljiro 4-ga brimmed with stores where people could outfit their apartments or houses exactly as they envisioned it. The first street I walked down was lined with wallpaper stores selling everything from the most traditional black and white checkerboard pattern to glittery purples and golds. Another road hosted almost nothing but furniture stores, with a special focus on chairs. If I hadn't already picked one up for my desk at home, or had I been competing in some sort of outrageous chair contest, I would have been in all sorts of luck. Metal lawn furniture? Check. Cow-patterned mini barstools? Covered. Red velvet armchair with gold accents and a two-meter-high back? Why, yes, your majesty, but the scepter is sold separately.

Whoever buys that last one will presumably need somewhere to store their treasure, and, fortunately, Euljiro 4-ga was also home to a collection of businesses selling safes. Those of the same style but different sizes were lined up next to each other like disassembled Russian nesting dolls, and while there were the obvious no-nonsense shades of silver and beige, some stores also offered safes in crimson on crimson floral patterns or with pictures of van Gogh's *Sunflowers* or Klimt's *The Kiss*, should you wish to incorporate a lockbox into your living room décor.

Lining Eulji-ro, particularly to the west of the station, were a number of lighting shops. Spotlights, track lights, chandeliers, metal lampposts—they were all there. The stores also included many unique styles unlikely to be found elsewhere (or in the average apartment), such as giant V-shaped ceiling lights or softly glowing orbs that looked like luminescent dinosaur eggs. The rest of the street was filled out with businesses for practically every DIY niche: metal banisters, pigments for mixing paint, tiling and bath stores with urinals and squat toilets lined up on the sidewalk for inspection.

The neighborhood had more to it than just house supplies, though. To the north, Baeogae-gil was lined with sewing machine shops, a vestige of the days when the area was filled with garment factories churning out the clothing for Dongdaemun's markets. Those factories are now long gone, but there are still businesses here that sell and repair not only desk-sized industrial machines but also equipment and supplies for home use. On the street facing the Cheonggyecheon Stream was a series of stores focusing on power tools, circular saws, drills, and jigsaws. One shop was devoted exclusively to pivoting wheels for flatbed carts.

The meandering Bangsan Market hid several more commercial islets. Within it was a baker's market with items you'd be hard-pressed to find anywhere else in Seoul, things like rye flour and molasses. There were cookie cutters and cake pans, too, and just about anything else a serious baker could want. Much of the rest of Bangsan was filled with small printing and packaging shops, and motorcycles zipped through alleys with their loads of paper or cardboard strapped to flatbeds rigged onto the bikes. Many shops focused on specialty packaging, with some devoted solely to stickers or clothing tags, while others might make, say, both the bags dog food gets sold in and the ones in which your new jeans are handed to you. My personal favorite was an oversized cloth shopping bag that read "LET'S BE PALSY-WALSIES" on the side.

Less specialized and more impenetrable was Daerim Arcade, a once-vibrant two-story shopping center that was now very run-down and mostly filled with shuttered businesses. I walked up a set of concrete stairs to the second level where, surprisingly, a small restaurant was open and, even more surprisingly, had customers. Weirder than that, though, was the glass display case outside that held stun guns and condoms, both of which, judging by the fading color on the boxes, had been sitting there for so long that the question of which was more dangerous was not entirely hypothetical. Euljiro 4-ga's slightly shabby mien and its highly specialized commercial offerings went some way to explaining why it had always been a little bit lost for me and why I had never ventured through before. These aspects also suggested that, unless I had the sudden need for a bathtub or muffin pan, I probably wouldn't be back anytime soon. I retraced my steps out of the Daerim Arcade and walked back through the furniture shops, past the station and sewing machine stores, and up to the Cheonggyecheon Stream. Even this best-known of Seoul landmarks had a more reclusive feel here. Lit up, accessorized, and often crowded where it begins near City Hall, it was calmer at Euljiro 4-ga, with fewer people around. I had it almost to myself. The water flowed around stepping-stones and past banks of reeds, starker, but no less beautiful in the winter, the tawny stalks brushed with fresh snow.

Key places: Furniture stores, lighting fixture stores, sewing machine and parts stores, Bangsan Market, Cheonggyecheon Stream, Daerim Arcade

BIFF! BAM! POW!

*The Saturday morning cartoon sights and sounds of
Seoul's commercial heart*

There are chickens in Myeong-dong. Not stuffed or fried, but real, actual chickens, about 10 of them, that twitch and peck at the dirt in someone's small yard, and if you got to the station early enough, before the neighborhood woke up and turned into its daily calliope of commerce, what you'd hear might not be the thump of dance pop and the exhortations of high-booted sales-girls, but the bewildered crowing of a rooster wondering where in God's name he's ended up.

Where he's ended up—in Seoul's main shopping district, with its crowds and neon lights and some of the world's highest real estate prices—wasn't always this way. In the postwar years, it would have taken a true visionary to imagine Myeong-dong as it is now. But like the city around it, the area has transformed, and to trace its development is to come to the conclusion that this single square kilometer may represent the diverging postwar fates of the two Koreas more fully than anywhere else on the peninsula. The area is everything the North is emphatically not: unabashedly international, hyper-capitalist, über-prosperous. At all hours of the day, Chinese and Thai tourists can be seen alongside (horror of horrors!) their Japanese and American counterparts, usually loaded down with shopping bags, eager participants in the white-capped churn of capitalism as millions of dollars are made and spent here every day. Which is why those chickens surprised me so much. They seemed like they would be more at home in some alt-history version of Myeong-dong, one where MacArthur's Incheon landing never happened, the North won the war, and Seoul became a dour expanse of factories and subsistence farming.

As it is, Myeong-dong has become perhaps the most bustling spot in an already notoriously bustling metropolis. On a weekend evening, roaming the streets feels like wading through a busy club with a particularly indecisive DJ—full of bumped shoulders and shuffle steps, with the song changing every 10 seconds as you pass through the waves of K-pop that emanate from storefronts. The music, the energy, the crowds, the flashing lights, the barkers barking in Korean or Japanese or Chinese—it will all either invigorate or drain you. For me, it does both. When I'm in the mood, there's nowhere in Seoul that's more exciting or that makes living in East Asia, with all its intensity and drive, more appealing. But when I'm not, I feel like a cartoon character who's just had his bell rung: woozy and disoriented, with flashing stars swirling around my head.

While much of the area is too caught up in its own consumerism to even notice, Myeongdong-gil is always a scene for street theater. Cutting through the middle of the district, this pedestrian street acts as a magnet not just for shoppers, but also for the curious, noisy, and eccentric. Tour groups donning matching hats trail behind their guides' bobbing pennants. Shoppers nosh at the many food carts. Christian proselytizers come with speakers to blare out hymns and exhortations of conversion, routinely ignored by everyone. Demonstrators air grievances, like the students from Dongguk University who were objecting to the closing of the Buddhist school's creative writing department not with noisy slogans, but by repeatedly prostrating themselves.

There is, in fact, a long thread of protest weaving through Myeong-dong's history, and that thread has frequently run east on Myeongdong-gil to Myeong-dong Cathedral. Stemming from its foundations as a sanctuary for Catholics in a country that was not always hospitable to them, the building has had a long association with dissidents and protesters, providing both a staging ground and asylum, most notably for pro-democracy advocates in the 1970s and '80s.

The cathedral was the largest building in the capital when it was constructed, in 1898, and its red-and-gray brick exterior features a 45-meter steeple with a gray-green peak and thin metal cross at the top. On the day I went, a Sunday, the walkway leading up the hill to the church was busy with people on their way to Mass. Out front, a small choir sang hymns. Inside, stately gray stone pillars met and formed the arches supporting a simple white roof. On either side, intricate and brightly colored stained glass windows allowed light in, and flanking the apse were large paintings illustrating Christianity in Korea. On a rear balcony was a massive pipe organ. For the moment it was silent, and the only sounds in the pre-Mass church were rustling papers, footsteps, and the noises of people settling into the pews.

For many, the name Myeong-dong immediately calls to

mind the area north of the station, but there is, of course, a neighborhood south of it, too. It's here that I found the Seoul Animation Center, the city's shrine to all things illustrated. While its animated products aren't nearly as well known as those of neighboring Japan, Korea is fertile ground for illustrators, and much of the work for numerous American series, including *The Simpsons*, is actually done here. Painted in bright colors (of course) and watched over by a statue of Taekwon V, the '70s-era world-saving robot, the center had whimsical dioramas, film screenings, and caricature artists in the lobby. Naturally, most of the visitors were kids, including one at a photo booth, straining to stand on his tiptoes to get the top half of his head in the frame, not quite realizing that he simply could have backed up a couple of steps. I was, I'm fairly certain, the oldest non-parent there, but despite that fact I spent the entire visit with a dopey grin smeared across my face. At no time was this truer than when I went to the bathroom. The back wall of each urinal was composed of a video screen that alternated between a target, a taunting fly, and an animated Whac-a-Mole.

Next to the Animation Center is the Cartoon Museum, which isn't quite so much a true museum as it is an animation archive. On the first floor is the Cartoon Library, offering shelves and shelves of comic books, manga, and graphic novels. Upstairs, kids and their parents were slouched in front of the dozen or so TVs, watching videos taken from the huge collection on offer, everything from *South Park* to Pororo (the little blue penguin in aviator goggles so popular here he's been dubbed the children's president) to the 1964 stop-motion *Rudolph the Red-Nosed Reindeer* Christmas special that I must have watched a gazillion times as a kid.

The area just west of the museum was almost quiet, at least in relation to its surroundings. Although hints of the more modern Myeong-dong existed there in the form of clothing and jewelry boutiques, it was still very much the sort of place where buildings had kimchi pots stacked outside, and it was there that I saw the chickens.

Do chickens dream of flight? If they do, those 10 in the dirt courtyard must spend their days envying and wondering about the oddly shaped gray birds that only ever trace the same path, back and forth between the bottom of the mountain and a white, silver, and red needle at its top. Flight is escape, and the Namsan cable car's ascent up to N Seoul Tower, at the mountain's summit, is at once an escape from the tumult of the city and a way to take it all in. Head up the tower and at its viewing platform there are no shoppers, no barkers, no protesters, no preachers. There is only the city as abstraction, as the metropolis Taekwon V flies over, as testament to potential half realized and half squandered, and, after the sun sets, as terrestrial galaxy, nowhere more luminous than the electric supernova below you.

Key places: Myeong-dong Cathedral, Seoul Animation Center and Cartoon Museum, Mt. Namsan cable car

TOPROCK

*The rise of the Korean b-boy, and how he helps keep
Olympic Park alive*

One of the first gifts I can remember loving to the point of
obsession was a red baseball cap that my aunt and uncle brought
me when they came back from the 1988 Seoul Olympics. It was
terrifically ugly, mesh with a stiff velvet front that stuck up like a
Russian army officer's hat, but that hardly mattered at the time. I
was 6 years old and oblivious to Korea, but I was enthralled with
the Olympics (two weeks of nothing but sports!) and I liked the
blue, red, and yellow swirl of the logo. There are few pictures of
me from that year without that hat on.

More than a quarter-century on, and with the hat retired to
a box in my family's basement, I found myself at the wellspring
of those childhood reveries: Seoul's Olympic Park. Unlike the
Olympic facilities of so many past host cities, Seoul has done

a reasonably good job of keeping its venues from turning into white elephants, an accomplishment that's certainly been helped by the fact that park space in the city is at such a premium. Besides Olympic buildings, the huge park holds museums, remnants of an ancient earthen fortress, a man-made lake, a segment of the Seongnaecheon Stream, and the huge 88 Field. While so many parks in Seoul have—quite maddeningly—fenced off their grassy areas, 88 Field is free for frolicking and is often filled with families picnicking and playing baseball or badminton.

The other thing staving off decay is the continued use of the facilities for sports, concerts, and other events. One of the biggest and most dazzling is the R-16 World B-Boy Championships and Urban Arts Festival, held every summer, often in Olympic Hall. This two-day event serves as the country's biggest showcase for Korean and international urban culture, and during the festival the area outside the hall is filled with portable DJ stands, clothing booths, and a large wall that graffiti writers from Korea, Hong Kong, the United States, and elsewhere transform into an al fresco gallery of international urban art.

Along with graffiti, the other three elements of hip-hop—MCing, DJing, and b-boying—have all fully become a part of youth culture here, the last one in particular being somewhere that Koreans have laid down a marker. While for a lot of people b-boying still calls to mind images of kids spinning on cardboard on sidewalks in the Bronx, Korea is now arguably where you'll find the world's best dancers. Crews from the peninsula have won six of the past eight R-16s and seven of the past 12 Battle of the Year events, b-boying's most prestigious international competition.

How did that happen, halfway around the world from the art form's origin? According to Benson Lee, director of the documentary *Planet B-Boy*, things began to take off in the late '90s, with the arrival in Seoul of a Korean-American b-boy named John Jay Chon. Although a b-boy microculture already existed in the Korean capital, Chon's influence and a video of a German dancer he brought with him that was copied and passed around hand to hand gave the movement the push it needed. What happened next—the country's subsequent rise and sustained success—Lee attributes to two other factors, one a manifestation of Korean society, the other a pushback against it.

"I think it's part of the Korean psychology of 'We've got to really succeed. We've got to make something out of ourselves,'" he told me. "And they took that sort of attitude and applied it to b-boying, and as a result they excel. I think there's just that common work ethic that exists in Korea, whether it's a cab driver or a guy delivering beer, whatever. This is a hardworking country. And this is the secret to Korea's economic rise, and I don't think you can exclude them, because they're in hip-hop, from that ethos."

That Korean work ethic is inextricably linked to a national Napoleon complex, to a need for recognition and approval, and to the suspicion that, no matter how much it achieves, Korea is still seen as a "small" country. Few crews in the world have excelled more or brought greater recognition over the past several years than Seoul's Jinjo Crew, but despite winning back-to-back R-16s and the 2010 Battle of the Year, the feeling that the message still wasn't clear hadn't gone away.

When I asked Kim Hyun-woo, Jinjo's best dancer, about his motivations before one R-16 event, he spoke as if he bore responsibility not just for his crew but for his country as well.

"Still there are some countries that don't know about Korea. This is a world competition and a lot of people will come, so I want to show my best."

Despite this recognizably Korean sentiment, the contradicting struggle to exist outside of society's strictures is the fire's other spark.

"In Korea if you're not sort of academically inclined then you're kind of brushed off here," said Lee. "And here's a form of art for these kids where they excel because they're really passionate about it and then they're recognized for their talents. So b-boys suddenly become like superheroes."

Which makes R-16 something like a convention where the Avengers, X-Men, and League of Extraordinary Gentlemen are all gathered in one place to determine whose superpowers are most super. Below DJ booths and a live band, and wrapped in a haze of old-school funk beats, the battleground for eight of the world's best crews is a meter-and-a-half-high stage where the dancers spin, flip, leap, and launch each other through the air. At its best, watching a battle can seem like a refutation of everything you ever learned in physics class, a perfect marriage of force and grace—a linebacker in pointe shoes, Baryshnikov with a sneer. As the battle ebbs and flows, alternating between subtler, more technical movements and virtuosic displays of skill, the noise from the audience does the same, until a particularly stunning move draws a collective punctuation of *Ohhhhh!* from the crowd that becomes as much a part of the aural setting as the bass lines emanating from the speakers. While b-boys' moves are performed *for* the crowd, they're performed *at* the rival crew, often occurring right in front of them, limbs flying centimeters from their faces. The second the battle is over, though, guards are dropped and embraces exchanged. Countercultures tend to engender fraternities, and b-boying bridges nationalities.

Indeed, before Chon showed up, Korea's first b-boys had begun by imitating the American G.I.s—from the Bronx and elsewhere—that they'd seen in Seoul's Itaewon neighborhood. Right around the time I was given my Seoul '88 hat, while the world was focused on the games that served as modern Korea's great coming-out party, that small coterie of misfits was discovering a new form of self-expression far from even the dimmest spotlight. Fast-forward two decades, and the next generation of those concrete artisans have become world champions, that street corner the bright lights of the national Olympic facilities.

Perhaps b-boying bridges eras too. At the second R-16 I went to, just before Saturday night's solo b-boy final, a troupe of *pungmul* musicians took the stage. *Pungmul* is a traditional music form of the Korean countryside, heavily percussive and imbued with physicality, and unlike more formal traditions its musicians dance as they play, twirling and twisting in time with the drums. When the troupe emerged, the lights dimmed and the decks stopped, and suddenly the only sounds in the hall were the players' drums—the *kkwaenggwari, janggu,* and *buk*—pounding out a much older rhythm. After a few minutes they were joined onstage by the Rhythm Monsterz crew. The DJs started spinning again, and the beats of the hip-hop classic "Apache" filled the auditorium, the *pungmul* musicians falling in, pounding their drums in time with the downbeat. As the b-boys and the drummers merged and flowed in and out of each other, I realized that there was a third reason for b-boying's unexpected success here. The union of beats and movement that defines b-boying existed in *pungmul* as well; b-boying was simply a modern reflection of a Korean mixture of sound and physicality with roots centuries old. Near the end of the act, the performers retreated to the back until only two were left. In the middle of the stage was a solo b-boy, his body vertical, hands pounding the floor, feet revolving above his head. Circling around him, a lone *kkwaenggwari* player—torso parallel to the ground, baton striking gong, legs windmilling through the air.

Key place: Olympic Park

PERIOD PIECES

Chungmuro's nostalgia for the past, in wood, stone, and film

At the top of the main set of escalators inside Chungmuro Station is a pair of walls covered in old photographs—shots of well-dressed people accepting awards, their time-faded colors actually making them look more dated than the older black-and-white film stills just around the corner. They're the first indication one gets of the area's close association with Korea's film history.

Some of the earliest motion pictures screened in Korea were shown in Chungmuro, and decades later many film companies set up their offices there. Recent years have seen the nexus of Korean cinema shift to the outskirts of Seoul and to Busan and Jeonju, but Chungmuro still holds more than just a nostalgic association with the silver screen. For starters, there's the historic Daehan Cinema. Founded in 1955, the Daehan is one of the oldest movie theaters in Korea, though you wouldn't know that by looking at it. Renovated and reopened in 2001, it's now a modern multiplex, and at night floodlights illuminate the multistory banners advertising the latest domestic gangster flick or Hollywood blockbuster.

More than other art forms, it's the visual immediacy of those two filmic cousins, cinema and photography, that lends them to flights of reminiscence, and the neighborhood's ties to them might go some way to explaining how deeply Chungmuro is steeped in nostalgia. Virtually the entire area south of the station is devoted to a dreamy-eyed look at the past, a film set without the film.

Near Exit 3 is Korea House, a *hanok* mansion located on the former site of the residence of Joseon-era minister Park Paeng-nyeon and built by Shin Eung-su, whose carpentry skills were designated an Important Intangible Cultural Property by the national government. Judging by the building, Shin earned it. The house is huge and gorgeous, its dark-brown wood exterior highlighted by vivid white paint. Stepping through the heavy front doors into a bright airy hallway revealed an inner courtyard, on the right side of which a pair of stone dragon heads spouted water into a square pool. Hallways leading back to rear dining rooms were blocked off by paper screens, but I could peer past some that had been left open and admire the lovely painted ceiling panels, separated by smooth wooden crossbeams and spaced with wood and paper lights. Inside a hall to my right, staff wearing traditional dress moved about an elaborately laid-out dining table, ferrying food or attending to one task or another. It was easy to imagine that I'd slipped back in time 100 years, or at least that I was on the set of a meticulously detailed period drama. And then, like an inattentive gaffer wandering into the shot, the auto-door to the men's restroom slid open and a guy ambled out, buckling his belt as he did so.

The lovely settings of Korea House function as a space to educate people about traditional culture, and visitors can view music and dance performances, experience court cuisine (if you feel like emptying your wallet—not cheap), try their hand at making kimchi, or learn to play the *janggu*, an hourglass-shaped drum. The typical modern Korean wedding takes place at a purpose-built wedding hall and is an assembly line–like affair that is often over and done in less than half an hour. But for those looking for something more than an in-n-out-you-want-fries-with-that? ceremony, Korea House performs elaborate traditional weddings too, complete with *yeonjigonji*, the circular red dots of makeup applied to the wife-to-be's cheeks, in case your blushing bride isn't blushing quite enough.

For much of the tradition without the price tag, there's Namsangol Hanok Village next door. The village's main feature is five *hanok* homes from different parts of Seoul that were either disassembled and moved there or re-created according to the original design.

Before arriving at the *hanok*, visitors come to a large central plaza where kids are often playing *gulleongsoe*, a game where they use a stick to push around a wobbling metal ring. To the left is an airy pleasure pavilion and performance stage, and at the back of the plaza is a second pavilion where craftsmen make various items from woven straw, including sandals, egg carriers, baskets, and *ttwari*, small pads to provide cushioning when carrying your water jug or—why not?—your camera jib atop your head.

The *hanok* section of the Hanok Village is a soothing palette of white, ivory, charcoal, ash, straw, and speckled gray, broken only by the cinematically contrasting green plants and strings of electric lights covered in rectangular red-and-blue cloth sleeves. The *hanok* themselves represent homes across a wide spectrum of income levels, and each interior is outfitted with furnishings and accessories as it might have been hundreds of years ago, making the village a good place for a starter course in premodern Korean life. Between the homes and the village's other features—walking paths, an artificial stream, man-made ponds filled with fish and water striders skimming across the surface—you could easily spend an hour or more lazily walking around, trying your hand at folk games like *tuho* (arrow tossing) or *paengi* (top spinning), or imagining yourself in a historical drama, delivering your lines in the most stentorian Joseon voice you can muster.

Like Korea House and the *hanok* in the Hanok Village, photographs and films are also acts of preservation; some aspect of the present is plucked from its anonymous existence so that it can one day serve as a representation of or story about the past. At the very rear of the Hanok Village, the Seoul Thousand-Year Time Capsule is buried. Curving paths lead from the top of a large grassy knoll down into a basin where the enormous cover of the capsule sits patiently, waiting to be opened on November 29, 2394, when Seoul turns 1,000. Until then, somewhere beneath it lie 600 items taken from citizen suggestions, buried on the same day in 1994, upon the 600th anniversary of the city's founding. Doubtless among them are photographs and films that, by their nature, will show future citizens of Seoul glimpses even further into the city's past than the container's other objects. Sitting on the capsule's cover, I could see the top of N Seoul Tower to the south, but to the north the city was cut off by the basin's rim, and all that was visible were clouds dangling in a broad and timeless blue sky, which, come to think of it, is a pretty good closing shot.

Key places: Daehan Theater, Korea House, Namsan Hanok Village, Seoul Namsan Traditional Theater, the Seoul Thousand-Year Time Capsule

BARISTAS AT THE GATES

Go away, nobody's home. Wait, you brought lattes?
Well, why didn't you say so?

Few areas in Seoul allow one the opportunity to see the city reshaping and reinterpreting itself as well as Hapjeong does. In particular, it offers a living timeline of the ways in which outside influences have been received by Koreans over the past two centuries, from the earliest Christians to the latest baristas.

To witness this in condensed form, all it takes is a short walk from the station to the Hangang River. On its banks you'll find Jeoldusan Martyrs' Shrine and Yanghwajin Foreign Missionary Cemetery, but the route there, particularly if you go via a back-street like Seongji-gil, will take you past a medley of foreign imprints that would have been barely imaginable 20 years ago, let alone a century: Western-style cafés, tart shops, a Vietnamese restaurant, a bike shop catering to local hipsters. It will also take you past the offices of Star Empire Entertainment, where, when I passed, a flock of two dozen teenage girls was waiting outside. I walked up to one of them and, in a pidgined mix of English and Korean, pumped her for information:

Me: "Why? Who's inside?"
Fangirl: "ZE:A!"
Me: "Who?"
Fangirl: "ZE:A. Idol group."
Me: "How long did you wait?"
Fangirl: "Two hours."
Me: "You come here every day?"
Fangirl: *Confused silence* (I take this as a *yes*.)

Unfortunately for all of us, but mostly for Fangirl, ZE:A did not come out. I left the studio and the magic marker professions of love for its employees scrawled on the walls and continued along to my original destinations.

Constructed in 1967, the Martyr's Shrine sits atop a bluff overlooking a bend in the Hangang River. In 1866 this was a major site of the Byeongin Persecution, the last of several such 19th-century purges of Korean Catholics, who were viewed as a threat to the state's Confucian ideology. The purge was ordered by the powerful Heungseon Daewongun, regent of the Joseon Dynasty and father of then 13-year-old King Gojong (r. 1863–1907), and its immediate cause was the seizing of Ganghwado Island, at the mouth of the Hangang River, by the French admiral Pierre-Gustave Roze, commander of the French Far Eastern Squadron. The seizure was a response to the execution of several French Catholic missionaries, which, in turn, was a response to their being neither welcomed nor invited by a country with a strict policy of isolationism. Not content with merely eliminating nearly half of the Catholics in Korea, Daewongun wanted to send a message, and with its proximity to the Yanghwajin Ferry Crossing and its popularity as a recreational spot, the bluff above the Hangang River was chosen for an execution site. Of the approximately 8,000 Catholics killed during the 1866 purge, nearly 180 met their end here, giving the place the name it bears today, Jeoldusan—Beheading Hill. In 1984, 103 of the martyrs killed here were canonized by Pope John Paul II at a ceremony held in Seoul, resulting in the odd footnote that South Korea has the fourth-highest number of saints of any country in the world.

Today, Jeoldusan's peaceful grounds house a chapel, museum, and numerous monuments to Korean saints and martyrs. Mass was being celebrated inside the chapel when I visited, and I was surprised both by how full it was on a Saturday afternoon and by the fact that many of the women—the older ones in particular—were wearing lace veils over their heads, an old-fashioned Catholic practice that I'd never seen before, despite having been raised in the church.

The shrine's museum displayed a small collection of artifacts related to the history of Catholicism on the peninsula, including the *Grammaire Coréenne*, the first grammar textbook for foreigners. There were also examples of small porcelain bowls that were buried with the recently deceased, as headstones were forbidden on the graves of martyrs. Outside were stone carvings of the Stations of the Cross and a towering statue of Andrew Kim Taegon, Korea's patron saint. There was also a raised bank of red, blue, and yellow votive candles nearby, and I watched a young boy gaze up at their flames for a long while, fascinated, then rise up on his tiptoes to try to blow them out. Too short; the prayers were spared.

A short stroll west was the Yanghwajin Foreign Missionary Cemetery, where a number of early expat residents are buried, a large percentage of whom were missionaries. In a rather ironic turn, it was King Gojong himself who designated this a site for the foreign proselytizers in 1890.

The cemetery sits on a small hill, and narrow footpaths run between gravestones, a number of which were chipped and pockmarked by bullets and shrapnel in the Korean War. The graves vary, from simple stone slabs marked "Unknown" to more prominent stones indicating significant figures in the foreign community's past. Among these are the journalist and Korean independence advocate Homer Hulbert, whose tombstone famously reads, "I would rather be buried in Korea than in Westminster Abbey," and Horace Grant Underwood, who founded Chosun Christian College, the precursor to one of the country's most prestigious academic institutions, Yonsei University.

After leaving the cemetery I walked back up Seongji-gil to see if the girls were still waiting outside. Two hours after I'd first passed, almost all of them had left, but the girl I'd talked to and her two friends were still holding vigil.

"No ZE:A?" I asked.

"No, not yet," Fangirl answered.

While the riverbank enshrines the past, the rest of the Hapjeong neighborhood is a case study in contemporary Seoul's forward momentum and its significantly more welcoming attitudes toward foreign culture. That character and the cosmopolitan vibe evident on Seongji-gil are even more pronounced on Yanghwa-ro 6-gil, commonly known as café street.

In the United States, brewing or buying coffee is just something you do in the morning, as automatic as brushing your teeth, so it was a rude awakening when I first came to Korea, in 2005, and found that here coffee was largely thought of as something one bought in packets, half sugar and half dusty tan powder. If I wanted to go to a café I had to take the subway to an entirely different neighborhood. In the past decade, however, coffee culture in Korea has undergone a sea change. From 2006 to 2011, the number of coffee shops in the capital ballooned by 900 percent, and I've lost track of how many acquaintances have said they dream of quitting their jobs and opening cafés.

My walk up Yanghwa-ro 6-gil, as the street's nickname suggests, demonstrated just how completely coffee has been embraced by Koreans, how rapidly it's transformed from something foreign to something that's at the same time a status symbol and taken for granted. What was particularly encouraging, and revealing, about Café Street, was that each café was independent and unique; these were places opened by locals embracing foreign culture, not enormous chains imposing their product in the search for a new market. (Of which there's plenty in Korea. Seoul has more Starbucks branches than any other city in the world.) Nor was it just the coffee scene this was happening with. Here you'll also find Japanese izakayas, an Indian curry joint, and Spacca Napoli, where Yi Yeong-woo bakes pizzas in an authentic wood oven, a skill he perfected while studying in Naples. Speaking as someone who used to live in Italy, what comes out of that oven is the real deal—maybe the best pizza in Korea.

The eagerness to adopt and incorporate foreign influences has helped make the greater Hongdae area one of the city's most unique and vibrant neighborhoods, but as it's become increasingly well-known and commercialized, its most interesting and idiosyncratic places have been pushed toward its edges, including the area around Hapjeong Station. Just how long the area will retain its independent character, though, is uncertain. Several years ago, plans were announced for an enormous mixed residential-commercial development on the northwest corner of Hapjeong Intersection. Included in the designs was a large HomePlus supermarket, which drew protests from employees and supporters of neighborhood grocers and markets; throughout much of the construction they camped out in front of the development in a show of disapproval. Today the protesters are gone, and the tower and its mall are open. Like the rest of Hapjeong, it too has plenty of foreign influence: UNIQLO, the Gap, the second Starbucks on the intersection.

Where does one draw the line between "good" foreign influence and "bad"? It's a question that Korea has dealt with for centuries, but answering is tricky and rife with opportunities for hypocrisy. Café Street's independent coffee shops are wonderful, but they only exist because Starbucks first popularized coffee here. Catholicism has provided solace and a sense of meaning for a great many Koreans, but Christianity also birthed numerous cults in the country that have engaged in abusive practices with their followers. The question is frustratingly personal, too. I sympathized with the protesters, and I want the neighborhood markets and the chipped tombstones and the old Korean houses. But I also want my Western comforts: coffee and a modern apartment and the Tesco breakfast cereal that HomePlus stocks. I want the past and I want the future. The trouble is that I want them both now.

Key places: Jeoldusan Martyr's Shrine and Yanghwajin Foreigners' Cemetery, Hapjeong café street

Geoyeo Station
Line 5

DOWN AND OUT IN GANGNAM

What the Miracle on the Hangang River left behind

From the sidewalk above I could see the entire neighborhood—a large swath of houses in various stages of disrepair, roofs covered with plastic tarps weighed down by spare bricks and tires, a dusting of snow across their tops. At least eight church spires poked into the sky. A small metal staircase led down into the neighborhood, and at the bottom, faint odors of urine and earth came from homes' outdoor toilets and the vegetables drying out on mats beside nearly every front door.

Even after living in the city for two years, I had persisted in the notion that Seoul was an almost uniformly prosperous place. Urban poverty in America, even in smaller cities, is a very visible thing, so much so that its manifestations—homelessness, drug abuse, violence, the projects—are just part of our idea of what a city is. If you're in a city, those things are there, of course. In Seoul, though, sure, maybe not everywhere was Gangnam, but just about everyone seemed to get by OK. Those markers of American poverty were missing. There weren't neighborhoods you went out of your way to avoid, and you could go days, weeks even, without seeing a homeless person. Whenever I did glimpse outright poverty of the sort I was used to seeing in U.S. cities, it was always individuals down on their luck, like the homeless that congregated at Seoul Station, not something that seemed firmly woven into the city's fabric.

Now here I was, in the middle of a slum, and I didn't know what to do with it. It didn't fit with my idea of the city, and although I'd ventured about as far as one could venture and still be in Seoul, beyond the Seoul Ring Expressway even, I was still in the wealthy Songpa-gu district, one of three that are generally lumped together when people talk about Gangnam. The Songpa-gu I knew was the one I had seen just across the street, on the west side of Geomi-ro, where the landscaped Seongnaecheon Stream curled through the neighborhood, lined with walking paths and manicured shrubs. There, people bought single tomatoes shrink-wrapped in Styrofoam from a gleaming supermarket and cross-trainers from the Nike store. Inside a pet shop, a poodle had been getting its hair cut and blow-dried. Here, in the neighborhood where I now stood, packing tape spider-webbed across cracked windows. Off the streets crisscrossing the neighborhood ran tiny alleyways, maybe a meter wide, strewn with small chunks of rubble and lined with homes covered in cheap linoleum siding. Clotheslines were strung between the homes, and several mailboxes, some of them just plastic jugs with their sides cut out, were stuffed to overflowing with unpaid utility bills. A bit further into the neighborhood I passed a wall where a piece of paper had been taped up. It advertised a two-room apartment for KRW 200,000 (USD 170) a month and read, a bit desperately, "If you call the number below you can view the place right away!" Not far away, a similarly sized place in a new building could cost five times as much. Stepping away, I noticed a dead rat on the ground beneath the sign, stiff and dry.

Not many people were around, and those I did see were mostly of retirement age. With a loosely meshed social safety net, a heavy reliance on children to provide for aging parents, and a society that's changed faster than many could keep up with, it's the elderly who most often face poverty in Korea. I wondered if they, or, in truth, anyone, was actually moving here, and if the people already here were trying or able to move out.

Back near the stairs was the Oryun Senior Citizens' Community Center, and inside, several old men were watching TV news, sitting cross-legged on the floor or half-absorbed into a fake-leather couch. The most talkative of the bunch, Gil Man-su was still handsome, with neatly parted hair, crisply pressed pants, and grayish eyes. As some men his age do, he stood with his shoulders thrust back and his hips slightly forward, giving him a posture like a boomerang. Though he'd recently moved away, he was back visiting friends in the neighborhood where he'd lived for some 30 years. I asked him who lived here now, and he estimated that 70 percent were retirees.

"Most people moved here from condemned neighborhoods, places that would be torn down," he said. "The rent's cheap here, and they didn't have enough money for other areas of town."

It was a story echoed by Choi Rak-jae, a realtor with a small office on the neighborhood's edge. Choi was gazing idly up at the TV when I walked in, and in the back, a half dozen guys were gambling on a Korean card game called Go-stop, some holding wads of cash in their hands. They looked to have been drinking. Choi served me a cup of instant coffee and, like Gil, explained that most of the people living in the area had been priced out of their old homes in Yongsan, Dongdaemun, and Changjin-dong due to reconstruction. Others had moved here from the countryside. Those who had been made to relocate had received little compensation and had gathered here and built small houses virtually overnight.

Business, unsurprisingly, was bad—just a handful of visitors a week and practically no sales. It had been that way for three or four years. Choi's face, dotted with liver spots, twisted into a grimace.

"I didn't want to work here, but a friend convinced me. I only said OK because I was sick and thought I was going to kick the bucket in a couple of years."

He hadn't, and it was now a decade since he'd taken the job. Back then, things had seemed a little more optimistic, real estate–wise. As other old guys came and went between the card table and the street outside, Choi explained that the area had been marked for redevelopment for a long time, since the 1970s in fact, as I'd later learn. When the idea was first mooted and in the periods when new apartment complexes were proposed, business had been all right. The problem for Choi was that these periods were regularly interrupted by others when conflicts of interest or changed policies brought things to a halt, as had happened recently after Park Won-soon was elected mayor.

"Now, if most owners don't want to sell, they can't rebuild," Choi explained.

Gil had mentioned the reconstruction plans to me as well, claiming that almost everyone in Geoyeo wanted to take the relocation money and finally be able to afford to leave. And given the chance, who wouldn't want to get out of that neighborhood, with its tumbledown homes and air of neglect, and move someplace better? In Geoyeo, however, the new rules intended to protect homeowners had had a perverse effect. Nearly everyone who lived here didn't own, but rented.

"But the owners don't want to sell," Choi said, "because then they won't get rent."

This left the neighborhood's residents unable to collect the relocation money they'd be offered in the case of redevelopment and therefore unable to afford to move. Even if redevelopment finally did go ahead, it was likely that their prospects would be little better. Living in a neighborhood as depressed as Geoyeo, one of the cheapest in Seoul, any relocation money they were offered would likely be insufficient to find new homes elsewhere in the city. That left the mostly elderly residents in limbo, left to eke out a living in a far-off corner of the city while they waited for others to decide their neighborhood's fate.

I thanked Choi for the coffee and stepped back outside. The sun and the temperature were beginning to drop. An exhaust pipe on someone's house was blowing steam into the December sky, and the stream of air moving through it created a hollow wail that seemed to encapsulate the melancholy feeling of the neighborhood. At least that was how I felt as I walked back to the station. But I was also surprised to feel something else, something not unlike the moment you see an unattractive aspect of your partner for the first time and realize—with a mixture of relief and satisfaction—that they've let their guard down and let you in. My early view of Korea's capital had been so filled by its successes— its infrastructure, its safety, its technology—that at times it felt flawless and fake, an android city. Geoyeo was a side of it I had been unaccustomed to and unprepared for, yet also a side that was recognizable. Its poverty was far different from the poverty of American cities—more benign, less violent, a problem rooted in generation, not race—but it showed me for the first time the tears in Seoul's urban fabric, and in a complicated way this made the city more identifiable, more relatable. Here I was in Gangnam, and although it was a part of Gangnam that would never make it into tourist brochures or viral videos, it was every bit as much a part of it as the Gucci stores and the gleaming skyscrapers, its residents every bit as much a part of it as the K-pop idols and the conglomerate scions. Suddenly, Seoul felt less like a place I merely found myself and more like the city I lived in.

Key place: Seongnaecheon Stream

UNFOLDING

Is it possible to ever truly know a place?

It should be obvious that in a city of Seoul's size there will always be a place that catches you unaware, that opens like a fold of paper in a game of Exquisite Corpse, revealing something at once recognizable and yet utterly, sometimes bewilderingly, unexpected. It should be obvious, what with the enormity of Seoul's population and expanse, but it isn't. One gets accustomed to one's surroundings, often remarkably quickly, and an idea of the city congeals. This is no less true for expats. The primary motive for those of us who move abroad is often the hazy promise of adventure, but, paradoxically, we also pride ourselves on how rapidly we adapt to the new surroundings, how quickly we can claim (with varying degrees of falsity) that we "know" the city, that it's all old hat. Call it the race to blasé. But then a fold lifts and you suddenly

feel like you don't know the city at all. For me, Sindang was full of these folds.

My first visit started familiarly enough: lunch with some friends at Sindang-dong Tteokbokki Town, a street devoted to restaurants selling the schoolkid favorite of pressed rice cakes in a spicy, slightly sweet sauce. The only thing that felt a bit off was that this was in the dog days of summer, and while there's never really a bad time for *tteokbokki,* it's undoubtedly best in the winter. That's when well-lit carts on dark streets are their most alluring, the steam pouring out into the cold air, wrapping the carts in an irresistible haze, and when you pull aside the flap and step into the pungent circle, the warmth of the food, the hot fish cake broth, and the bodies packed in next to you help you forget about the cold for at least a few minutes. Unfortunately, my friends and I had to settle instead for the entreaties of restaurant pitchmen and an August haze that left us deliciously tormented by the bubbling sauce and steaming rice cakes.

After eating, I walked across Toegye-ro to the shiny glass-and-steel façade of Chungmu Art Hall. In the upstairs gym, several girls' volleyball teams were holding practice, while on the first floor, visitors browsed through a photography exhibition and bought tickets for *Rent.* Outside, bright red, green, orange, and yellow chairs shaped like globs of melting taffy sat on a lawn of fake grass. The gimmick was likely intended to make the hall seem "greener" and more inviting, but all it did was remind me of how badly the city lacks the real thing.

Modern structures like the art hall or the nearby restored Cheonggyecheon Stream are the exception in Sindang, however, contrasting sharply with much of the rest of the area, which can be decidedly, stunningly archaic, filled with folds upon folds of the unexpected and the mystifying.

Just west of Chungmu Art Hall, the south side of Toegye-ro was lined with woodworking shops, and the smell of sawdust filled the air as I walked over the shavings sprinkled on the sidewalk. On the north side was a trio of blacksmith shops with outdoor racks where finished products hung: saws, stakes, hoes, rakes, hooks and picks and trowels and sledgehammers, along with many unrecognizable things that looked like their only possible use would be by very bad men to do very bad things. Each languished in various stages of rusting. Living in a first-world country, it's easy to forget that blacksmiths even exist anymore; the profession seems medieval, something from the realm of artisan guilds and knights-errant. Yet there they were, on a major downtown avenue, the same one that just a few blocks away passed in front of the entrance to Myeong-dong, one of the glitziest and most developed areas in the city.

I walked past slowly, peering into shops. In one, a smith with a pocked red face gazed out at the street, the burning embers of the forge glowing red-orange and illuminating the dim interior behind him. In another, Hyeondae Workshop, a second man sat watching a UFC match on a small TV set high up on a shelf. He looked as if he could get in the octagon himself, his thick torso and broad shoulders filling out a T-shirt dotted with tiny holes and brown stains. He introduced himself as Kim Yong-gyu, and as we began to talk he pointed to the bar in back where he did pull-ups. I asked how old he was, and was taken aback when he said that he was 74.

Kim started blacksmithing in the 1970s, teaching himself. "About 10 blacksmiths were here in the past," he said, "but that number is getting smaller because no one wants to learn. If there's any more development of this area the rest will close. It makes me a bit sad." Kim's voice was oddly cheerful as he said this, suffused with the good nature of the Buddhist at the gallows. He knew that his was a dying profession, but also that there was nothing to be done about it.

Unsurprisingly, business was scarce. Though big companies would occasionally come looking to buy custom pieces, or Kim might send material abroad when someone built a traditional Korean house overseas, he mostly passed his time reading books and studying English. As he showed me the shop's forge I noticed a whiteboard hanging up on the wall, an English phrase of the day written on it:

How would you like youre eggs? sunnyside up

"There's a small mistake here," I told him. "Would you like me to fix it?"

"Yes, yes, please," Kim answered and peered over my shoulder as I took my finger and erased the extra *e*.

If the Toegye-ro blacksmiths raised one fold, the area around Jungang Market unfurled like a paper fan, revealing an area of the city that felt at odds with the rest of Seoul and that made me feel more displaced than I had in a long, long time.

In the past, I'd been only vaguely aware of Jungang Market's existence. Despite being Seoul's third-biggest market and having handled 80 percent of the rice traded in the city at one point, it's almost entirely ignored by the English press; neither the Korea Tourism Organization nor the city of Seoul has an entry for it on its English website. Whether it's the cause or the effect of that lack of exposure, Jungang is strictly a locals-only place.

What I saw when I visited was a Korea that hadn't changed terribly much in the past few decades. The market extended far in front of me, motorcycles ferrying produce up and down the main aisle. There was pork, beef, dog meat, chicken breasts, chicken wings, and chicken feet. Seafood stalls held fish, shrimp, squid, and great piles of oysters. Round bags of kimchi, inflated by fermentation, brought to mind fishing bobbers—their bottom halves red and the tops colorless. Walking through the market, I began to have the odd, creeping sensation of being in a foreign country—an odd sentiment for an expat, perhaps, but my scales of banality about the city were falling away. I didn't know about this place. It wasn't like the Seoul I knew; it was earthier, more insular, somehow different. It was strange to me and I felt strange in it.

My sensation of displacement only grew as I walked through the area between the market and the Cheonggyecheon Stream. Whiffs of epoxy coming from a concentration of furniture shops filled my nose. Huge sacks of rice were piled to the ceiling in the small one-room warehouses of grain wholesalers. Dogs kept six to a cage outside butcher shops slept curled up next to one another or gazed out at the street. The stores of the Hwanghak-dong Kitchen Furniture Street sold every kitchen supply imaginable, domestic or industrial. Small inns dotted passageways. Workers lined up at sewing machines in tiny clothing factories. Gritty restaurants were jammed into minuscule alleyways where shop awnings created a canopy above the lane.

What was couched away between station and stream felt virtually unrecognizable to the high-tech, appearance-conscious picture of the city that non-Koreans generally carry, and that many Seoulites do as well. It felt cut off not just from the guide-book world but from the rest of Seoul, like a remote island where unique and bizarre species have evolved.

A bit further north, between Majang-ro and the Cheonggye-cheon Stream, things got even more curious, in the remnants of the old Hwanghak-dong Flea Market, where a strange pantomime of commerce takes place. Every day, stalls open for business and lay out offerings that it's hard to imagine anyone ever buying: costume jewelry, typewriters, rotary phones, fake steer horns, two-decade-old stereos, Super Nintendo game cartridges, Laurel and Hardy piggybanks, dirty movies on VHS, burlap in three-meter-long rolls, ice buckets, tacky pirate statues, the sort of décor you'd find on the walls of small-town American bars. Over the course of several visits to the market, I don't recall ever seeing any deals being struck, leading me to wonder who actually shopped there, and how the sellers managed to stay in business. Could it possibly be worth it to come here every day to try to sell a quarter-century-old video game? Or was it simply a mix of habit and lack of other options?

Standing just outside the market, at the corner of Nangye-ro and the Cheonggyecheon, was an enormous new Lotte Castle apartment complex, complete with an attached Starbucks and an E-Mart, which is sort of the Korean equivalent of Wal-Mart. This was a more familiar side of Seoul, and yet after having disappeared into the market for so long, it was just as unsettling as the market initially had been. The two—the market and the apartments—seemed to be different worlds, as foreign to each other as I was to Korea. I wondered how many of the people who worked in the market lived in the high-rises, and how many of the people who lived in the high-rises ever shopped in the market. I doubted that it was very many at all.

There was one more surprise that Sindang held for me, this one underground. Just inside the main entrance to Jungang Market was a sign for the Sindang Raw Fish Center, accompanied by a picture of a fish painted in bright segmented colors like a stained-glass window. Next to it was a second sign, reading "Seoul Art Space Sindang." Down the ramp and past a string of sashimi restaurants were dozens of bright, clean artists' studios, most with finished work on display. There were hand-stitched leather bags, custom-designed baseball bats, and whimsical household goods designed to confuse—kettles shaped like radios and pencil holders like rolls of toilet paper. In a glass display case was a matchbox-sized book with translucent pictures embedded in the pages, like something a fairy might read.

In one of the studios was Oh Hwa-jin, who created sculpture-dolls by wrapping felt cloth around shoes or candelabras or other objects, resulting in pieces that looked like Muppets as imagined by Guillermo del Toro.

"I don't know what it will be when I start," she said to me, describing her process. "I discover the story as the piece develops."

That description, I thought, could apply equally to Sindang. This was a neighborhood where first encounters hid as much as they revealed, and where things seemed to take form in unusual ways. Take, for example, the space we were in. As the Jungang Market's economy contracted, shops began closing and retailers in this underground extension left behind dozens of vacant stalls. The city government saw this as an opportunity, Oh explained, and as part of a series of Art Spaces around town, it converted the old market stalls into studios to support local artists and attempt to revitalize the neighborhood. Some of the desired effects were readily apparent, like the beautiful fish sign outside and the columns lining the arcade's hallway, which had been turned into a charming tribute to the sashimi restaurants' staff—covered with lenticular images of the workers, they turned from ordinary cooks and waitresses into Superman or Wonder Woman at the tilt of your head. I asked Oh if the arcade was having an effect beyond just the décor, and she seemed to think so. "People are getting to know about the Sindang area and bring development, which is good."

In a sense, it was good. Sindang was noticeably underdeveloped compared with many areas of Seoul, and things like Chungmu Art Hall and Seoul Art Space Sindang indisputably benefited the neighborhood. I had to wonder, however, whether plans to breathe new life into the area might have unintended effects, if the efforts to revitalize the local economy might result not in the resurgence of Jungang Market and other local businesses, but in moneyed and opportunistic interests seeing the development as a chance to further expand their reach, as the Lotte Castle complex suggested. The pattern occurs everywhere— big corporate entities move in, local shops get priced out—though with an economy that's so lopsidedly dominated by a few enormous conglomerates it tends to take on a particular speed and ruthlessness in South Korea. Should this happen again here, Sindang's small businesses wouldn't be revived—the folds veiling its mysteries would be ironed smooth one by one until nothing was hidden. When I returned a year later, the artists and the market were still humming along, and a new apartment tower was going in on the edge of the flea market. Kim Yong-gyu, as he'd predicted, had taken down his pull-up bar, packed up his whiteboard, and closed the doors of Hyeondae Workshop for good.

Key places: Sindang-dong Tteokbokki Town, Chungmu Art Hall, Cheonggyecheon Stream, Jungang Market, Seoul Art Space Sindang

INDUSTRIAL ARTS

*Work it, make it, do it, paint it, build it, shape it,
dance it, play it*

Once upon a time, there was a man named Mun who wore clothing made of hemp. Nearly all Koreans did at the time. Mun was a civil servant of the Goryeo Dynasty, and one day, Mun was instructed to board a ship and sail across the sea to perform duties as an envoy to Yuan China. In China, Mun saw fields of plants topped with flowers made of snow. He saw some laborers pluck these flowers from their stems and saw others spin the flowers into a cloth softer and suppler than the hemp garments he wore. Mun desired to bring the plant back to Korea with him, but he faced a problem: the plant was deemed so valuable that the export of it or of its seeds was banned. Mun was determined, though, and eventually he found a merchant willing to do business. In a quiet spot, Mun discreetly paid the merchant and slipped a handful of seeds into the hollow of his writing brush. He then tucked the brush into his bag, got in his boat, and sailed back home, smuggling the seeds out of China. When he returned to Korea, Mun planted the seeds in the earth. Before long, they grew, sprouting flowers made of snow that Mun harvested and spun into cloth. Koreans had never before seen such plants or felt such cloth, and everyone asked what the plants were and how they'd gotten there. They asked so many times that after a while the explanation ceased to be just an explanation and became the name of the place where the cotton plants grew: Mun-lae, or, "Mun came here."

It's almost certainly apocryphal, this Promethean story of how Mullae got its name, but it's also rather apt, as hundreds of years later Mullae would once again be closely linked with fabrics. For centuries a waterlogged patch of earth just south of the Hangang River, the 1930s saw several small textile factories built here. A community sprang up around them and was named Saokjeong, meaning "thread-making village." According to a second story, after World War II, the village's Chinese name was dropped in favor of a purely Korean one, a name that meant "weaving loom": Mullae.

Regardless of which story is true—or if neither is—taken together they trace the arc of Mullae's progression, from the undeveloped to the agricultural and from the agricultural to the industrial. That arc is what we call Development, and it's hardly unique to South Korea, but what sets the country apart from so many others is the intensity with which it occurred here, as the nation went from sub-Saharan levels of poverty to the world's 15th-largest economy, all in the span of 60 years. It was a leap in which Mullae played an outsized part. The post-Korean War development boom replaced many of the thread-making village's textile factories with manufacturing and machine shops, turning the area, along with much of the surrounding Yeongdeungpo-gu district, into Seoul's engine room, pumping out the tools the city would use to build itself. That building and rebuilding, that invention and reinvention, has been the story of the city ever since, as it tries to figure out what it is and what it wants to be. This process and the laser-like speed with which it happened have created a legacy of dynamism and a city where modern developments and lifestyles exist side by side with those a half-century old, sometimes complementing, sometimes clashing. It's a phenomenon that's apparent in practically every part of the capital, but, as I found, perhaps nowhere is it as bluntly visible or as ongoing as at its source.

In the area immediately surrounding Mullae Station, the sidewalks were lined with leafy, gentrification-friendly trees, apartment complexes in affirming shades of beige, and shiny glass office towers with coffee chains on their first floors. A short walk east was a new mall with an indoor waterpark. Just across the street, however, the earthy smell of onions, garlic, and mud emanated from a long row of stores where men and women in their 60s and 70s sat on crates next to their merchandise, prices scrawled in marker on scraps of cardboard beside them. Standing on the corner, I could take in the wholesalers, the mall, the squat brick apartment buildings, and, in the distance, the shimmering towers of a new shopping complex—a half-century of urban development in one glance.

The iron muscle for some of those structures may not have come from very far away. Southwest of the station was a warren of streets lined with one-story manufacturing shops. Walking through it, I could smell wood shavings and grease, and the whir and thud of machinery pounding metal provided a rhythmic soundtrack. Sections of the ground were littered with tiny glinting shards of steel, as if a mirrorball had exploded. Men in tank tops unloaded metal weights shaped like oversized cow tags from a truck. A man and a woman stood examining a slightly rusty J-shaped tube the circumference of arms held out in an empty hug. Occasionally the man would take out a torch and weld or bang at something with a hammer, then pause to inspect his work.

Southeast of the station the air had a different smell: the acrid tang of heated metal coming from other, larger factories housing intimidating, room-sized machines. In one workshop, slabs of metal the width of two pool tables lay stacked on top of each other, and in another, workers placed long sheets of steel 10 centimeters wide into a huge machine that bent them 90 degrees. Elsewhere, long iron rods of different sizes and colors were organized in enormous shelves like pastels in an art supply store. The scene was utterly alien to the image of Seoul put forth in guidebooks and tourist brochures, despite being in many respects the source of that image. Seeing things here felt like peeling back the skin on an android to uncover the gears hidden beneath.

By producing the raw material that Seoul needed to transform itself from postwar wreck into world-class city, Mullae's manufacturers were at the same time pricing themselves out of town. As the capital developed and real estate prices skyrocketed, many manufacturers decamped to the provinces or overseas, leaving unused factory space behind. But one man's abandoned factory is another's potential studio, and beginning about a decade ago, artists, encouraged by the city government, began moving in, taking advantage of cheap rent or merely appropriating abandoned buildings and setting up workspaces, creating Mullae Artist Village.

Unlike other Seoul neighborhoods with high concentrations

of artists, Mullae isn't a place where you can simply show up and gallery-hop. There are a handful of exhibition spaces, but the neighborhood is primarily a place where artists work, with private studios interspersed among the remaining machine shops. Walking through the streets around the factories, one notices graffiti, wall murals, and installations—like one of the headless white mannequins perched on a rooftop—but to really get under the skin of the scene requires knowing where to look or having someone show you around. This was something I didn't have the first time I visited, and I left thinking that the Mullae artistic experiment was failing, or was at the very least overhyped.

My second time around, I met with Jason Mehl, an American sculptor who worked out of a shared second-floor studio on Dorim-ro. Mehl greeted me at the door dressed in a Mooney Suzuki T-shirt and a tweed pageboy that was fraying around the brim. Several of his studio mate's paintings leaned against the walls or lay on the floor, and on the balcony outside hung one of Mehl's works in progress: a large oblong form, tan and scarred and pocked with holes. It made me imagine the autopsied lung of a chain-smoking whale. Once Mehl was satisfied with the sculpting, he'd cast it in bronze and ship it home to Texas.

We talked about the neighborhood for a while, and Mehl described a more vibrant place than I'd first perceived, remarking on its homey feel, the group meals the artists had, and the work that went into the community. But he also harbored some ambivalence about Mullae and about Korea's art scene. There wasn't enough integration between Korean and foreign artists in the neighborhood, and Korean art students, despite having exceptional technical skills, were stymied by constantly being told "no." "There's an expectation of what to make and what not," Mehl said. Another impediment was the outsized emphasis placed on which school students studied at, common in all professions in Korea, and although this was less emphasized in Mullae, it still carried some weight. The area was full of talented artists, Mehl said, but they might not make it due to where they graduated. "Most of these people will never be accepted."

We left the studio to take a walk through the neighborhood. A light rain had started to fall. It was quiet except for the occasional burst of sound coming from a studio or factory, and Mehl pointed out some of the artwork hidden in the alleys. There was something fairy tale-ish about walking through those corridors in the rain, as if the creations of Lewis Carroll or J. M. Barrie had slipped through tears in the fabric and into the post-Industrial Revolution world in which they'd been dreamed up. Amid the grays something bright and whimsical would pop up, a cheerful robot or a daydreaming cat, like it was hinting at a playful world just beyond my sight. Or something dark and foreboding would seep out from the walls, like a mural of Little Red Riding Hood's pursuing wolf, adding a penumbra of menace to the already gloomy day.

Without a personal guide to Mullae's art scene, there are two good starting points to discovering the neighborhood. The first is Seoul Art Space: Mullae, one of several such Art Spaces established by the city. The one here occasionally holds performances, and there is studio and exhibition space for musicians, dancers, and woodworkers. Perhaps the most unique artists working at the Mullae space when I visited were Project Nalda. "Nalda" means "to fly" in Korean, and the troupe used ropes and harnesses to perform swooping, swaying vertical dances along the sides of buildings.

Aside from the Art Space, the most accessible gateways to the Mullae community are the numerous café-galleries that dot the neighborhood. Though it's since closed, for a long time one of the most important of these was Cottonseed Café. In the scene's early days, Cottonseed was the only exhibition venue outside the Art Space, and after meeting with Mehl I headed there to pay a visit to Kim Jeong-hee, the café's manager. A pretty, youthful woman, on the day I met her Kim was wearing a baggy periwinkle shirt, intricate silver rings, and chipped blue nail polish. She explained the scene's origins and the effects of the influx of artists into what had previously been a strictly industrial area.

"At first, the factory workers didn't like it. It was an annoying thing. The factory workers had to work hard and they thought the art looked like garbage." This changed over time, she said, as the machinists saw what the artists did, and eventually the two groups began collaborating, the workers providing technical advice and tools, the artists creating public works to enhance the neighborhood.

Similar to the relationship between the machinists and artists, Mullae's exhibition spaces also worked together to collaborate on exhibits and foster the community. (When Cottonseed closed it was bought by a local artist and turned into another café-gallery, Café Suda.) Kim described the members of the Mullae scene as a family, and on the day I visited Cottonseed, Kwon Bo-seon and Yun Sang-beom had made that analogy literal, occupying the café as part of an installation piece, transforming the gallery into a public living room. Initially studio mates, the couple later married, living and working together. Eventually, though, the owner of their studio had asked them to move, and the conversion of the café from exhibition space to home was meant to memorialize their former studio.

Contrary to the impressions of my first visit, the art scene seemed to be thriving, but it was also facing new questions,

poised to transform again. Mehl had mentioned that he felt Mullae was already changing, with artists moving out into cheaper areas as the neighborhood got more expensive and "official." Many of the emptied studio spaces were being or had already been turned into restaurants, and the neighborhood's location, between the business hub of Yeouido and the upmarket Mokdong area, made it an attractive proposition for real estate developers, raising the possibility of more exhibitions like Kwon and Yun's in the future.

"Mullae has a big problem, and that's reconstruction in the area," Kim said. Both Seoul and the Yeongdeungpo-gu Office had their eyes on the neighborhood, hoping to replace many of its small structures with yet more towers, insisting that it would be better for the local artists to work in more modern environs. Unlike in more practical-minded parts of the city, however, Mullae possessed a skeptical attitude toward development. Kim and the artists I met liked the current Mullae just fine. They felt at home in the old brick buildings and ex-factories hidden down narrow alleys, nostalgic for the way things were. Kim sighed a bit and looked out the window before speaking again. "Walking around here is like a time machine to the '80s."

Key places: Small manufacturing shops, Mullae Art Village and industrial area, Seoul Art Space Mullae

ODD WORLDS

Over the river and down the rabbit hole

The area around Yangjae Station is one of those rather anonymous Gangnam neighborhoods of wide avenues, utilitarian office buildings, and businesspeople lugging briefcases. But as if it formed some sort of mystical barrier, cross the Yangjaecheon Stream to the south and odd worlds start to open up.

I went across the stream and followed it as it flowed west, first passing alongside cherry trees and forsythia that burn yellow in the spring and then going underneath the growling ceiling of a highway. This brought me to Culture and Art Park and Alicepark, an Alice in Wonderland–themed park that, when I visited, sat abandoned. This was the spring of 2011, and though a banner at the north entrance reading "Hello Alicepark 2011" implied recent desertion, things looked as if they had been sitting untouched for much longer, as if, with no one to keep an eye on them, time and entropy had seen an opportunity to run wild. Detritus had piled up inside ticket booths. A wooden-shoe house, hollowed-out apples, giant mushrooms, and an enormous mosaic-cat house all stood in dilapidation. I wandered past playing-card soldiers that guarded nothing at all; unrelieved of their posts, they continued to keep watch. Further in, I stepped into a long canopied tunnel where a row of wild-branched wooden chairs sat forgotten, the empty thrones of a deposed fairy-tale council.

Theme parks are designed to evoke a fantastical world, and when you go to Disney World or, in Korea, Everland and buy a ticket, you're in a way agreeing to renounce the real world for a time. The park tries to create a place where the normal rules don't apply, where the unexpected and uncanny can happen, and you with your cotton candy and mouse ears buy in. You want to play along, so you act how you never would in the real world, surrendering control of what happens in a way you normally never would either. The fantasy is only heightened if the theme park has been abandoned. At Disney World, you can't ever completely fool yourself; you know there's a man inside the mouse. But at the forgotten Alicepark, that knowledge was gone, and the fantastical felt more wild, more real, as if Oz had left his creation to its own devices. With the queues and the stewards absent, and with even the park's abnormal rules dissolved, relinquishing control made me feel as vulnerable as it did liberated. There were no smiling mascots to welcome me, and so I wasn't sure if I was welcome. Stumbling into Alicepark by chance, I felt not unlike Chihiro in *Spirited Away*, and when I left it felt not so much an exit as an escape.

After making it out, I went further south, to the point just before where the city gives way to highwayland. There, gray-green peaked roofs marked Yangjae-dong Flower Market, the largest in Korea. Here, too, stepping into the greenhouses was a bit like walking through a magic door, only this time instead of transporting me into a fairy tale ghost town, it opened onto, say, rural Brazil. Temperature and humidity hovered around 25 degrees and 26 percent, and a dense green scrim was spangled with vivid bursts of pink, yellow, and magenta. Heart-shaped anthuriums were so red they looked spray-painted, and miniature Venus flytraps somehow managed to be both adorable and menacing at the same time, like a newborn vampire. The scent that filled the air inside the greenhouse was pure, and breathing in almost felt like an act of cleansing.

But on the south side of the Yangjaecheon Stream, even in a temple devoted to all things natural, I was still unable to escape the otherworldly entirely. In the northwest corner of the market was a mélange of objects you could buy to decorate—if that's the right word—your garden: topless faux Grecian busts, miniature windmills, life-sized giraffes, and giant dragonflies on five-meter poles. Walking through the area was like meandering around the set of an especially bad (or amazing, depending on your tastes) B movie.

Between Alicepark and Yangjae Flower Market was Yangjae Citizens' Forest, built for the 1986 Asian Games and the largest man-made forest in Seoul prior to the creation of Seoul Forest. In the center of the park was the Yun Bong-gil Memorial Hall, dedicated to the man who threw a bomb at a Japanese army celebration of Emperor Hirohito's birthday in Shanghai on April 29, 1932, killing two Japanese officials and wounding several others. He was summarily arrested and executed in Japan, but in 1946 his remains were exhumed and reburied in the Korean National Cemetery. The memorial hall exhibits some of Yun's belongings and features a simple exhibit on his life.

The south end of the park was the site of three additional memorials, dedicated to the Korean Army's 9th Infantry Division, nicknamed Baekma, which fought in the Korean War; the victims of the 1995 Sampoong Department Store collapse; and the victims of the 1987 bombing of Korean Air Flight 858 by North Korean terrorists. It was also, unexpectedly, a popular spot for cosplayers to hang out and photograph each other, thanks to the periodic conventions Seoul Comic World hosts at the nearby aT Center. Like a lot of people, I had associated cosplay with Japanese *otaku* culture and the alternate universe of Harajuku and was unaware of its presence in Seoul, so stumbling upon this heavily made-up subculture here was unanticipated, but, given what I'd already experienced in Yangjae, not exactly surprising.

Though Yangjae would never be mistaken for Harajuku—and, in fact, Korean cosplayers must frequently deal with dirty looks or disparaging remarks from those with anti-Japanese sentiment, as several cosplayers told me—the kids seemed at home here and added a jolt of whimsical, quirky life to a park that, thanks to its collection of memorials, was a touch morbid. A stocky high-schooler wore a Gundam costume he'd made himself, fashioned from cardboard and full of moving parts; an American cosplayer wore the puffy pink dress of Super Mario's Princess Peach; and a girl with iceberg-blue hair and matching dress twirled a delicate parasol. There was a pair of friends dressed up in matching bright-blonde wigs and heavy eye makeup, versions of a Japanese pop star who's a humanoid persona of a singing synthesizer application and sometimes performs concerts as a hologram. (Got that?) There was Victorian gothic and video game, manga and mutant, samurai and superhero. Depending on their characters, the cosplayers were alternately charming, serious, brooding, or bubbly, done up with hair extensions and chiffon and leather and lace and chains and wigs and jewelry and enough eyeliner and eye shadow to power Broadway for a month. Standing there, I started thinking that maybe it wasn't the world south of the Yangjaecheon Stream that was odd. Maybe, in my jeans and T-shirt, it was me.

Key places: Yangjaecheon Stream, Alicepark, Yangjae Flower Market, Yangjae Citizens' Forest

MIXED MEDIUM

The jumble of sights and sounds of Seoul's center

If there's one station that can claim to be Seoul's center, the nexus from which everything expands and to which it returns, it's Jongno 3-ga. For centuries, Jongno has been the principal thoroughfare of the Korean capital, the avenue that linked the city's east gate with its main palace, was paraded down by Joseon nobility, and saw the city's first skyscrapers. The section denoted 3-ga sits at its heart, surrounded by tourist attractions, financial offices, remnants of the city's royal heritage, and a smuggler's den of specialty shopping areas.

Like so many other travelers, Jongno 3-ga was where I began my first visit to Seoul, emerging from Exit 1 and slipping in among the throngs of locals and sightseers crowding the sidewalk. I've been back countless times since, and despite now living in the city, whenever I return to the station I almost invariably find myself tracing the same path I did on my first day, the well-worn trail west down the sidewalk to the tourist hub of Insadong.

The route there passes in front of Tapgol Park, a small patch of concrete dotted with trees and gazebos, all wrapped within a tile-topped brick wall. The park's centerpiece is the stunning 10-story marble Wongaksa Pagoda, which is currently encased in a giant glass box to protect it from the elements, making it look a bit like a hugely magnified version of the souvenirs sold in the nearby tourist shops. Opened in 1920, Tapgol was the city's first modern public park. The previous year, this location had also been the site of one of 20th-century Korea's most celebrated events, the reading of a declaration of independence from Japanese colonial rule on March 1, 1919. Sadly, it was a declaration that was largely aspirational, as the peninsula would have to wait until the end of World War II to reclaim sovereignty.

Outside the park's western wall, the sidewalk is lined with a dozen or so square tents, each just big enough to hold a small table and two or three plastic stools. Inside are fortune tellers who, for a few dollars, will offer glimpses of the future through tarot cards, palm readings, or *saju*, a traditional East Asian method of fortune telling based on the time and date of a person's birth. At dusk, bare fluorescent bulbs in each of the tents switch on, and the glow spills out onto the darkened sidewalk.

Just beyond the fortune tellers is the entrance to Insadong-gil, the pedestrianized road that's the center of downtown tourism. Pause before going in, though, and you'll see a tiny alleyway beneath a wooden sign off to your left. The sign's Korean script reads "Pimatgol Pub Village," and the alley is what's left of the historic little corridor of Pimatgol. Much as it is now, Jongno was the main thoroughfare of Seoul during the Joseon Dynasty and the principal route for nobility and government officials moving through the city. Whenever they did, astride their horses, standard bearers announcing their arrival, any commoners on the street would have to prostrate themselves until the big men passed or risk punishment for failing to show the necessary deference. This was obviously a drag, and to avoid the inconvenience commoners took to using the narrow alley running parallel to Jongno, which at some point was given the name Pimatgol, or "Fleeing the Horses Alley." Thanks to the heavy foot traffic, dozens of restaurants and pubs sprang up along the corridor, transforming it into one of the most bustling, vibrant concentrations of blue-collar life in the capital.

Like so many other places, though, the alley fell victim to urban redevelopment, beginning in the 1980s. Where the hoi polloi once shuttled back and forth for much of the length of Jongno, eating, drinking, and no doubt making jokes about the men on horses, there are now mostly skyscrapers, with several incorporating public, ground-level walkways in a sterile imitation of the old passage. Only the area immediately west of Insa-dong, with a few small bars and restaurants wedged into the nooks, bears any resemblance to what Pimatgol once was.

Most tourists, however, pass by oblivious to the old alley, eager to get to Insadong-gil's galleries, cafés, and souvenir shops. Despite Insa-dong being tourist central, I never find the camera-toting visitors bothersome or the neighborhood best avoided in the way I find many cities' tourist hubs. I actually like going there, and from conversations I've had with locals their general feeling is similar. Why is this? Some of it stems, I think, from the fact that Seoul isn't yet a tourist town to the extent that cities like Tokyo and Bangkok are, and so the number of visitors it gets isn't overwhelming. (Although this has been changing, in large part due to increases in the global reach of Korean pop culture and the portion of the Chinese population with the means to travel abroad.) It helps too that Insa-dong's current character is threaded to its past as a center of the antique trade and to its postwar status as the city's focal point of artistic and café culture. But the main reason I think Insa-dong has weathered its emergence as a tourist district reasonably well is that it doesn't cater to tourists at the exclusion of locals. Insadong-gil itself may have witnessed some unfortunate changes in recent years, like an influx of chain stores, but off the main street the alleys are still filled with old tea shops and wood-beamed restaurants. And unlike in so many cities' tourist districts, the food and drink at these places are actually quite good, meaning they're typically crowded with locals while the tourist surge carries on just a few meters away. It's possible that I may give Insa-dong too much credit for what authenticity and tradition it retains simply because these things have been either destroyed or sacrificed most elsewhere in Seoul, but the fact is it remains a place where side street convenience stores advertise not souvenirs but cigarettes and trash bags.

Jongno 3-ga's other major tourist attraction is Jongmyo Shrine, constructed in 1395 under the direction of King Taejo to house the memorial tablets of the Joseon Dynasty's deceased kings and queens. Though the tablets have survived to the present day, the original building was destroyed by Japanese invaders in 1592. The current structure is still remarkably old, dating from 1608, and on Jongmyo Shrine's 600th anniversary, in 1995, the shrine was designated a UNESCO World Heritage Site. Rites honoring the spirits of the deceased royalty are still performed there annually on the first Sunday in May and are open to the public.

The shrine and its grounds are remarkably peaceful compared with their contemporary surroundings. Dirt paths wind between trees and ponds, and birds chirp in the treetops. The atmosphere is matched by the lovely but austere buildings, architecturally similar to those found in the royal palaces, but with none of their colorful and intricate ornamentation. Buildings here hew to a consistent burgundy-and-mint color scheme, reflecting the solemnity of their purpose. Connecting Jongmyo Shrine's structures are raised, three-part stone walkways—the outer lanes reserved for the king and crown prince, the central one for the spirits.

At Jongmyo Shrine, each past king's tablet is grouped together with that of his wife (or wives). An auxiliary hall, Yeongnyeong-jeon Hall, holds the memorial tablets of King Taejo's ancestors and some lesser Joseon kings and queens, but the majority reside in the *jeongjeon*, or main hall. Divided into 19 rooms, one for each king enshrined there, the hall is a long, one-story wooden building with a sloped black tile roof as tall as the story it covers. In front of the *jeongjeon* is a wide stone plaza, and if you stand in it the only things visible above the foliage are N Seoul Tower and the upper reaches of a single building a few blocks to the east. These, of course, were not around 600 years ago, and the visual quarantine was meant to preserve the tranquility of the memorial and to prevent worldly matters from intruding on the king's thoughts as he performed the ancestral rites.

The area in front of the entrance to Jongmyo Shrine is now a prettily landscaped park of shrubs and walking paths, but not so long ago it was a serious old boy hangout, where dozens of elderly Korean men gathered to do elderly Korean man things, like playing go. On one day I visited there were close to 100 games going on, providing a background clicking of stones so constant it was like listening to an orchestra of metronomes. Those not playing watched, practiced calligraphy, or took turns speechifying to a small crowd through a mobile PA system.

While the area just in front of Jongmyo Shrine has been spruced up and sterilized, the streets between the shrine and Tapgol Park continue to look like an al fresco retirement home. Walking around, just about everyone appeared to be over 60. The first time I passed through, there was something else that felt a bit off, and it took a few moments for me to realize that I'd had similar sensations before, in Cairo and Tangier: There were virtually no women around; almost the only ones I saw were those serving food and drinks to the many men out getting their kicks in the surrounding restaurants, bars, karaoke rooms, and love motels. Retired and with nothing better to do, many of the old men seemed to simply spend their time here getting drunk. Several were slumped over plastic tables or up against Tapgol Park's brick wall, empty rice wine and soju bottles around them, giving the scene a sour, abject air—a picture of how not to grow old.

Local demographics are also tipped by the fact that the area is part of Seoul's small gay scene, with several bars here discreetly marked with rainbow flags or "members only" signs. Though attitudes are changing, homosexuality remains stigmatized and poorly understood in South Korea, and the small area north of Jongno 3-ga Station is one of very few places in the city where gay men can be out comfortably. While younger gay people usually head for the neighborhoods of Hongdae or Itaewon, establishments here cater to an older crowd. Considering the proximity between the gay bars and the nearby alcoholic excess, one wonders if any of the area's drinking is the result of men trying to escape the stresses of a society that often fails to accept them or if they are merely odd couple neighbors.

Between the gay bars and Insa-dong is Nakwon Arcade, and when I visited and opened the door to go inside I was met with the wail of a soprano drifting down the stairwell from somewhere up above. Covering two floors, much of the building is devoted to the Nakwon Instrument Shopping Center. Wandering through, I caught snippets of people testing out violins, harps, flutes, and drums, like the bursts of a radio with its dial set to "scan." As I passed from someone drawing a bow across the strings of a cello to someone else peeling off riffs on an electric guitar, I thought about how moving through the streets of Seoul isn't all that different, and just how rare it is that you're not exposed to ambient music in this densely populated and always-on city, whether it's pumping out of a cell phone shop or seeping out of a subway rider's headphones.

The Nakwon Instrument Shopping Center is just one of several specialty shopping areas in the vicinity of Jongno 3-ga Station. On Jongno proper are the jewelers that make up the Jongno Jewelry District, and, behind them, backstreets host wholesalers and gem cutters where congeries of stones sit in little trays, the colorful unset tabs looking like tiny buffed pieces of rock candy. Along the north bank of the lush Cheonggyecheon Stream, a string of small shops sell emergency and safety supplies like traffic cones, fire extinguishers, alarm bells, and flashing red lights. Between Exits 12 and 13, some tiny alleys hold several science supply stores, their windows full of beakers, droppers, dials, scales, mortars, pestles, microscopes, and spiral tubes. East of that is a watch and clock market where, at small, greasy booths, men doing repairs poke at the innards of watches with tiny little tools, small selections of new timepieces laid out for sale before them just in case the patient dies on the operating table. Shop walls are covered with clocks—analog, digital, cuckoo—like some sort of German rail conductor's fever dream.

Slightly further east, across from Jongmyo Shrine, used to be Seun Greenway Park. For a time this patch of land looked like a swath of lush Jeolla-do province farmland that had been scooped up and airlifted to downtown Seoul. Along the sidewalk were stalks of gold-green rice, their heavy tops bowed over like question marks, and when the breeze picked up it would shake them and produce a barely perceptible rattle. I remember strolling down a walkway between two different varieties of millet, brushing my hand against their dried leaves as dozens of dragonflies flitted above. The park was just one section of an overambitious plan hatched by former mayor Oh Se-hoon to create a greenbelt running from Mt. Namsan to Jongmyo Shrine, but given Oh's 2011 collapse—due largely to the fact that "overambitious" was an adjective that applied to just about all his plans—it was always questionable whether it would ever be more than a quixotic little curiosity.

Ultimately, it wasn't. The park was removed, and current plans call for a stepped plaza linking the street with the run-down Seun Arcade. That building, and much of the surrounding area, is jammed chock-full of electronics shops. When I walked through the arcade, I felt as if I'd been shrunk down and beamed into the innards of some giant machine. Some things were easily identifiable—TVs, CD players, walkie-talkies—but most I had no clue about, thousands of oddly shaped pieces with wires and dials and switches and insect-like appendages. They were mysterious, like little plastic and metal magic charms. Maybe they did amazing and sophisticated things, or maybe they just helped make toast. It was like seeing 1,000 puzzle pieces but having no clue what the puzzle looked like or even if the pieces all belonged to the same image.

In many ways, this part of Jongno feels the same, a mélange of disparate parts that might coalesce into a whole, but then again might not, and after seven years of living here I'm still not sure which it is. In Jongmyo Shrine's leafy enclave, the spirits of Korea's past kings lay in repose, while just outside its walls skyscrapers are filled with workers who don't have a moment to rest. Development raises buildings that destroy a historic alley and then attempt to re-create it. A park replaces a concrete plaza, while right across the street a concrete plaza replaces a park. Customers walk out of jewelry stores with shiny new purchases in pretty velvet boxes, and others bring dull old watches to the clock market in the hope that the right tweak might restart them. Tourists shuttle back and forth, from Jongmyo Shrine to Insa-dong and from Insa-dong to Jongmyo Shrine, while on the route between an old man lies passed out on a bench. This city—is it one puzzle, or 1,000?

Key places: Tapgol Park, Insadong-gil, Pimatgol, Jongmyo Shrine, Nakwon Instrument Arcade and Nakwon Market, Jongno Jewelry District, Cheonggyecheon Stream, science supply shops, watch and clock market, Seun Arcade, electronics shops

ACKNOWLEDGEMENTS

This book is the unexpected result of a much larger, much longer project of countless hours and kilometers spent exploring one of the world's biggest cities. As such, it's hardly been a solo effort. First and foremost, I'd like to thank Elizabeth Groeschen for starting the Seoul Sub→urban project with me, helping get it off the ground, and devoting so much time and effort to photographing its many corners. A special thanks also to Meagan Mastriani, Merissa Quek, Joshua Davies, and Chris da Canha for their photographic contributions to the project and for making the city come alive when my words come up short.

In more personal terms, I'd like to express my gratitude to my family for their love, encouragement, and forbearance of a son and brother whose roaming takes him farther away than most. Closest to my heart, my deepest thanks to Soyi Kim for her love and support and also for always good-naturedly being whatever I might selfishly need her to be: translator, researcher, fact-checker, travel partner.

Lastly, thank you to the people of Seoul, who have always made me feel welcome and have always been tolerant of the nosy stranger wandering through their city.

Credits

Author   Charles Usher
Photographer   Robert Koehler

Publisher   Kim Hyunggeun
Editor   Shin Yesol
Copy Editor   Eileen Cahill
Designer   Cynthia Fernández